TING TANG MINE

&

OTHER PLAYS

NICK DARKE

A METHUEN PAPERBACK

A METHUEN NEW THEATRESCRIPT

First published in Great Britain as a paperback original in the Methuen New Theatrescript series in 1987 by Methuen London Ltd, 11 New Fetter Lane, London EC4P 4EE and in the United States of America by Methuen Inc, 29 West 35th Street, New York, NY 10001.

Printed in Great Britain by Expression Printers Ltd, 39 North Road, London N7

British Library Cataloguing in Publication Data

Darke, Nick
    Ting tang mine: and other plays.——
    (A Methuen theatrescript).
    I. Title
    822'.914   PR6054.A695/
    ISBN 0-413-17930-3

CAUTION
This play is fully protected by copyright. All rights are reserved and all enquiries concerning the rights for professional or amateur stage productions should be made to Margaret Ramsay Ltd, 14a Goodwin's Court, St Martin's Lane, London WC2N 4LL.

TING TANG MINE

Ting Tang Mine was first performed at the Cottesloe, National Theatre, London on 23 September 1987. The cast was as follows:

SALATHIEL TRENANNIGAN	Barbara Jefford
JAN MAY	Robert Glenister
GONETTA BATE	Lesley Sharp
LISHA BALL	Ralph Fiennes
HAILSHAM	Leslie Sands
GRAN	Joyce Grant
MAUDE MAY	Di Langford
RUTTER	Antony Brown
THOMAS MAY	Peter Halliday
ANNE ROSCROW	Hazel Ellerby
ARTHUR MAY	Jay Villiers
SENARA	Robin McCaffrey
COLAN	Craig Crosbie
MOSES HARVEY	Paul Hastings
CAPTAIN	Alan Towner
TREFUSIS/TRICE	Paul Kiernan
SANTO	Wayne Morris
BETTY ELDER	Laura Calland
KITTO	Grafton Radcliffe
RAW	Jim Millea
YSELLA	Caroline Wildi
PREACHER	Alan Towner
BLAKE	Paul Hastings
SOAMES	Wayne Morris
HOYLE	Jim Millea
MARTYN	Grafton Radcliffe

Directed by Michael Rudman
Designed by Carl Toms
Costumes by Lindy Hemming
Music by Matthew Scott

Production Note

Ting Tang Mine is set in Cornwall. The Cornish are a Celtic race, in character more canny than the Scots, less lyrical than the Welsh, closer to the Irish but most akin to the people of Britanny. They speak fast with a hard, unmusical accent. Their soft consonants are voiced, so the word butter would be pronounced 'budder' and not 'bu'er' as Captain Birdseye might say it – this is the most important feature to consider when speaking the language of this play. A native of Cornwall, when heard for the first time is frequently mistaken for an American, but he or she is *never* asked if they come from Somerset.

Author's Note

Ting Tang Mine, originally titled *The Earth Turned Inside Out*, started life as a community play, written for the Borough of Restormel in Cornwall. The play was directed by Jon Oram, had a cast of 100 speaking parts, and 1,500 local people were involved in the production. It received 12 performances in Penrice School Hall, St. Austell in December 1984.

ACT ONE

Summer 1815.
A bell rings, and MINERS, *including* THOMAS *and* ARTHUR MAY, *and* LISHA BALL *gather at the foot of the* COUNT HOUSE *steps. They carry picks, gads, boryers and bunches of candles. They wear helmets.* BAL MAIDENS, YSELLA, SENARA *and* GORLOS *arrive carrying large hammers. They stand around in groups.* GONETTA BATE, *a girl of indeterminate age, appears at the top of the hill overlooking* TING TANG *and shouts down:*

GONETTA: Waterloo's won! Boney's crushed! Mr Prussia's on 'is knees! Brittannia rules the ways!

TOM: How far d'ya walk to tell us that?!

GONETTA: Brigan Mine!

TOM: Oo sent ya, Shanks?

GONETTA: Coulda bin!

TOM: Then tell im Mr Bonaparte stopped off ere on 'is journey down the South Atlantic for ounce a copper, but found none!

GONETTA: No tin neither?!

LISHA: No tin neither!

GONETTA: What e look like, Boney!

ARTHUR: Giant chap, wi' two eads! Picked 'is teeth wi' shovel 'ilts! Ad knees as big as Prussia's!

RUTTER, *the* MINE CAPTAIN, *appears on the* COUNT HOUSE BALCONY *at the same time as* GONETTA *is joined by a party of* BRIGAN MINERS. ARTHUR *shouts at* RUTTER, *indicating the* BRIGAN MEN.

ARTHUR: We'll not work with these men Mr Rutter!

LISHA: Arm yourselves! Shovel 'ilts!

YSELLA: Pick a rock to sling at em!

RUTTER: Who're you?

RAW: Brigan men!

GONETTA: Sober, skilled and lookin for work!

YSELLA: Then emigrate!

SANTO: We eard you ad a copper lode wide as the Ganges!

GONETTA: We eard today was count day!

LISHA: Send em off Rutter!

GONETTA: Come on thun!

MRS ROSCROW, *principal adventurer in* TING TANG MINE, *joins* RUTTER *on the balcony. Her presence calms the miners.*

ROSCROW: Who are these men?

RUTTER: They're tributers from Brigan Mrs Roscrow, come to bid for work.

ARTHUR: We'll not work pitches with these people.

TOM: There's too many men chasin too little work, the prices will be set too low!

YSELLA: We won't have em on this bal!

SENARA: See em off!

YSELLA: Break their heads!

ROSCROW: Wait! We have a lode, the Great North Lode, which at this time is in bonanza. There are plans to prosecute the sett towards Nanphysic and deeds have been signed with Sir Richard Crabbe giving us leave to undermine his land. New shafts are to be sunk, and the sett worked back along the existing . . .

ARTHUR: Be worked out in a week!

ROSCROW: That is a risk my fellow adventurers that I have decided to take.

LISHA: That lode wun't last.

ROSCROW: It shows signs that it might.

LISHA: Who the hell advised y'on that one?

ROSCROW: Good advice was sought . . .

LISHA: Rutter! Spale the bastard for tellin lies!

ARTHUR: Wide lode like that could stop dead in a fathom, ask any bloody tributer and e'll tell ya that!

SANTO: Start the biddin!

LISHA: No!

ROSCROW: Mr Rutter, would you auction one pitch?

RUTTER: Jonas Hawken's pitch.

ROSCROW: At what price did this pitch sell last month?

RUTTER: One and eight.

ROSCROW: Thank you.

A tense silence while RUTTER describes the pitch.

RUTTER: Jonas Hawken's pitch from the laddder winze so far east as Halebeagle shaft, from the back of the thirty fathom level so high as to join Amos Nicholl's pitch . . .

LISHA (*interrupting*): Ten bob a ton!

RUTTER: Too high Mr. Ball. I've set this pitch at five shillin a ton . . .

RAW: Four'n six a ton!

TOM: Four bob!

LISHA: I'll dig it for three and nine!

SANTO: Three bob!

RAW: Two'nine!

TOM: Two'n six1

ARTHUR: One'n eight!

RAW: One shillin!

LISHA: Christ! Ear that?

SANTO: Sixpence!

LISHA: Fourpence!

ARTHUR: Thruppence!

SANTO: Tuppence!

TOM: One penny a'penny!

RAW: One penny!

Silence. LISHA throws his pick to the ground and appeals to ROSCROW.

LISHA: Penny! A penny bloody pitch!

RUTTER calls up to RAW.

RUTTER: What's your name son?

RAW: Raw.

RUTTER throws a pebble in the air. They all watch it drop to the ground. When it falls, RUTTER says:

RUTTER: Raw. Taker. You wanna draw 'sist

ARTHUR: You can't dig ore at a penny a bastard ton!

ROSCROW: You work the tribute system because it gives you the freedom to come and go as you please. You own your pitch and if you don't like it you can bid for another next month or go to another bal. You're free to come and go! These men are too!

TREFUSIS steps forward.

TREFUSIS: We're different people to these, Mrs Roscrow. We dun't mix wi' Brigan people. They'd mix with the Polgooth crowd and we're more inclined to Trewhiddle. You gotta mix with a man when you're underground else you're forever lookin back to see if e gotta pick aimed at your head.

TOM speaks to the BRIGAN MEN.

TOM: Will you people leave us to Ting Tang if we swear an oath?

GONETTA: Oath to what?

TOM: Oath that we will never cross the river into Brigan and bid against you when your mine start producin copper again.

GONETTA: On what will you swear this oath?

TOM: Book of Revelation.

RAW: Go on thun!

ROSCROW and RUTTER go into the COUNT HOUSE.

TOM: (*looking round*): Didn't bring no militia with ya did ya?

GONETTA: No.

TOM swears an oath. As he does so, the MINERS melt away, till by the end TOM and TREFUSIS are the only ones left.

TOM: . . . and cast him into the bottomless pit, and shut him up, and set a seal on him that he shall deceive the nations no more til a thousand years be fulfilled . . .

TREFUSIS: Christ in hell that's some oath Tom. Thass an oath not to be broke Tom. There id'n no bugger gonna tinker with that oath. Ezekiel woulda sent em off Tom, or the booka Job, Revelation? Thass a desperate oath Tom. Christ in hell Tom, thass some oath.

TOM goes. TREFUSIS sings:

SONG
Thomas May and his son Arthur,
Dig cathedrals underground,
They wield their cross and mitre
Where copper can be found.

Their reward is not in heaven,
But closer down to hell,
Where night is everlasting,
And the devil rings the bell.

Inside the COUNT HOUSE, *a long table is set with a white cloth on which are the remains of a sumptuous meal. Round the table sit the* ADVENTURERS *in* TING TANG. *They drink brandy and smoke cigars.* ROSCROW *enters the room with* RUTTER, *who stays in the doorway.*

ROSCROW: Continue the bidding now Captain.

RUTTER *goes. A bell can be heard, off.* ROSCROW *sits at the head of the table.* HAILSHAM, *one of the* ADVENTURERS, *speaks.*

HAILSHAM: What's goin on?

ROSCROW: A disturbance Mr Hailsham. Some men from Brigan but they've gone now.

HAILSHAM: Good.

ROSCROW: Gentlemen, if you'll allow I'll call upon Mr Trice to proceed with the July samplings, read the accounts, and pay us our dividends.

TRICE *stands and opens a* COST BOOK, *he prepares himself.*

HAILSHAM: Get on with it.

TRICE: Gentlemen and lady. Ting Tang Bal . . .

HAILSHAM: Mine . . .

TRICE: I beg your pardon Mr Hailsham?

HAILSHAM: I adventure in a mine, not a bal, we'll have none of your vulgar slang here Mr Trice.

TRICE: Ting Tang Mine is in bonanza. I'm pleased to tell you that the Great North Lode is running rich and wide. Sadly we learned today that Brigan Mine, five miles distant, has ceased operation . . .

HAILSHAM: Come on, bugger Brigan . . .

TRICE: Thank you Mr Hailsham . . .

HAILSHAM: And you can dispense with the samplins, skip onto the accounts . . .

TRICE: That is out of order sir.

HAILSHAM: I'm a very busy man.

TRICE *looks at* ROSCROW, *who shrugs.*

TRICE: Accounts for the month ended . . .

HAILSHAM: Thass better.

TRICE: Accounts for the month ended July 31st 1815. Gross income was £4213, fifteen shillins and no, pence. Now to detail expenditure I shall start with contracted labour, at grass . . .

HAILSHAM: Do you ave to?

TRICE: Would you care for me to *sing* it to you Mr Hailsham?

HAILSHAM *laughs.*

HAILSHAM: Like to see y'damn well try!

TRICE (*sings*): Agents including pursers and clerks,
Ninety shillings and no, pence.
Contracted labour working at grass,
Eighty shillings and no, pence . . .
Twenty tutworkers, eight kibble-landers,
Two head smiths and nine binders tenders,
Carpenters, sawyers, smiths and pitmen,
Two hundred shillings and no, pence.
Three smiths' strikers and one bal captain,
Twelve bal maidens and eighteen whim men,
Eight hungry horses and three dozen children,
Twenty-two shillings and no, pence.
The total contracted labour expense,
Is three hundred and ninety-two shillings
And no, pence!

All the ADVENTURERS *clap except* HAILSHAM.

HAILSHAM: Huh. Er's a penny for ya.

HAILSHAM *flips a coin at* TRICE.

TRICE: Thank you sir. I shall move onto the tribute miners. The total tribute paid by us to the tribute miners was forty-one pounds, one shilling and no, pence. I think it in order to congratulate Captain Rutter, who is outside, for his accuracy with the July settings, when the potential of the Great North Lode was still in doubt.

The ADVENTURERS, *except* HAILSHAM, *clap.*

TRICE: The highest tribute paid was to Thomas May, who raised one hundred tons from the twenty fathom level with a pare of six men. In order to achieve this remarkable weight of stuff, Thomas May worked no less than twelve . . . (*He checks the cost-book.*) forgive me, thirteen doublers . . .

The ADVENTURERS, *except* HAILSHAM, *clap.*

TRICE: And was paid three pounds, ten shillings and no, pence. Lowest tribute paid was to Moses Harvey, whose pitch crossed the Cauter lode on thirty-two fathom level west. He grossed one pound, six shillings and no, pence . . .

HAILSHAM: Damned slight lode.

TRICE: Cauter lode is slight sir, yes.

HAILSHAM: How many ton of ore did e raise?

TRICE *consults the cost-book.*

TRICE: Thirty-two and a half ton sir.

HAILSHAM: Huh. Damned slight.

TRICE: Shall I continue?

HAILSHAM: How many doublers did this Moses Harvey work for 'is thirty-two and a half-ton?

TRICE: None sir.

HAILSHAM: Was e spaled for absence?

TRICE (*calls outside*): Mr Rutter!

HAILSHAM: Never mind Rutter I'm askin you.

TRICE: Not that I know of Mr Hailsham.

HAILSHAM: Did e work full cores?

TRICE: So far as the records for the month tell us yes.

HAILSHAM: I don't trust records.

TRICE: Would you care to go down and judge the pitch for yourself sir? It's hard ground and Cauter Lode is barren, we have Captain Rutter's word for that . . .

HAILSHAM: These lodes are barren with rich bits between. How do I know e idn' followin a string of quartz with bunches of ore here and there and e's leavin 'is best

work behind and covering it with deads on settin day?

TRICE: Moses . . .

HAILSHAM: So when Captain Rutter re-sets the pitch at a higher rate of tribute, up it all come to grass and Harvey Moses . . .

TRICE: Moses Harvey . . .

HAILSHAM: Earns hisself a bastard fortune! Bin done before . . .

TRICE: Not here at Ting Tang Mr Hailsham.

HAILSHAM: How the hell d'you know?

TRICE: Captain Rutter . . .

HAILSHAM: Mr Rutter id'n God Mr Trice.
Mr Rutter id'n Jesus. Mr Rutter, Mr Trice, knows not the stations of the cross and Harvey is Moses in nothin more than name!

HAILSHAM *turns and addresses the* ADVENTURERS.

HAILSHAM: There's too many loopholes in the tribute system! Money finds its way into the wrong pockets! I move, whilst the Great North Lode is rich, that we put the tribute miners under contract and pay em by the day.

ANN ROSCROW *interrupts quietly.*

ROSCROW: We don't work like that here.

HAILSHAM: Listen to me. You got Brigan Mine exhausted, you got men returning from the wars, the parish is rotten with idle men. Boney's defeat will knock the market for six, prices will plunge Madam!

ROSCROW: Why don't you sell your share?

HAILSHAM: Eh?

ROSCROW: A good speculator knows when to sell, by your estimation the time is perfect.

HAILSHAM: By my estimation no bugger'd be daft enough to buy!

ROSCROW: I would.

HAILSHAM: What price?

ROSCROW: Name one.

HAILSHAM: Four undred pound.

ROSCROW: I'm sorry Mr Hailsham,
I can't offer you more than three hundred
and ninety-nine pounds, nineteen
shillings and eleven pence.

HAILSHAM: Hah! Then I don't accept!

TRICE *flips the coin back to*
HAILSHAM.

TRICE: Here's a penny for you Mr
Hailsham.

HAILSHAM: I'm a dangerous man to plot
against.

TRICE: I assure you sir, we're quite
spontaneous.

HAILSHAM: I'm a man of substantial
property. I deal square. But when I'm
tricked on I turn devious.

ROSCROW: I've made a generous offer,
dealt quite square.

HAILSHAM: I'll have my broker draw you
up a contract.

HAILSHAM *storms from the* COUNT
HOUSE

TRICE: Well Mrs Roscrow. That gives you
a controlling interests in the mine.

The ADVENTURERS *clap and
disperse, taking their table with them.*
TREFUSIS *sings:*

TREFUSIS: Now some say Mrs Roscrow
Made Hailsham look a fool
He strode out pretty steamin
And kickin like a mule.

And I say if a woman
Cuts a foolish man to size,
His fury clouds a narrow mind,
He'll never more be wise. . .

GONETTA BATE *stands on the*
BRIGAN *side of the river which divides*
TING TANG *from* BRIGAN.
HAILSHAM *approaches the* TING
TANG *bank.*

GONETTA: Waterloo's won, Boney's
crushed,
Mr Prussia's on 'is knees,
Britannia rules the ways.

GONETTA *holds her hand out across the
river.*
HAILSHAM *is removing his shoes and
socks.*

HAILSHAM: What's your name?

GONETTA: Who're you?

HAILSHAM: Here's a penny.

HAILSHAM *flips a coin across the river
to* GONETTA.

GONETTA: Notta shillin?

HAILSHAM: You from Brigan?

GONETTA: I'm from Brigan.

HAILSHAM *has removed his shoes and
socks. He rolls his trousers up and wades
into the river while* TREFUSIS *sings:*

TREFUSIS: From Halifax to Hindustan,
From Alpine peak to Baltic town,
There's rivers deep, rivers wide,
Rivers dammed and rivers dried.

But this little river, duckfoot deep,
This lazy trickle, half asleep,
This teardrop on a mountain's cheek,
Got all the other rivers beat.

No Indus, Nile, Po or Rhine,
Cut so deep a boundary line,
As the one this river does define,
Twixt Brigan Bal and Ting Tang Mine.

HAILSHAM *has reached the* BRIGAN
side of the river.

HAILSHAM: What's your name?

GONETTA: Gonetta Bate.

HAILSHAM: Take me to Brigan.

GONETTA *leads* HAILSHAM off
towards BRIGAN.
TREFUSIS *stays where he is.
The atmosphere changes.* JAN MAY
*appears as if from nowhere. He is dressed
in a bizarre mixture of exotic clothes, all
slightly too small for him. Loud check
trousers, a military coat with gold braid
and huge epaulets. A scarlet shirt with
frills, multi-coloured chocker, a mis-
shapen 'Napoleon' hat, and a bright
yellow handkerchief cascading from his
pocket. He wears a riding boot on one foot
and a gentleman's walking boot on the
other. He carries a bulging carpet bag. He
reaches the* BRIGAN *bank of the river,
and looks around him, as* TREFUSIS
sings:

TREFUSIS: Have you never bin to Egypt?
It's a short day's walk that way.
Have you never seen a Pharaoh King?
Then set eyes on Jan May.

Have you never seen a peacock?

With its feathers in full fan?
Then look across the river,
And set your eyes on Jan.

Have you never seen a jackass?
Or heard its empty bray?
Don't look any further,
E id'n far away . . .

MAUDE MAY, JAN'S *mother, appears on the* TING TANG *bank of the river. She is dressed as drab as* JAN *is bright. She removes her boots and hitches up her skirt as* TREFUSIS *sings:*

TREFUSIS: And this extravaganza,
Tis all about Jan May,
Who crossed the parish border
On his Mother's back one day.

MAUDE *starts to cross the river.* JAN *notices her.*

JAN: Mother? That you Mother?

MAUDE *stops and looks up.*

MAUDE: Jan? Oh Jan! Aw, my darlin boy! My Jan!

MAUDE *crosses the river while* TREFUSIS *sings:*

TREFUSIS: From Mexico to Jabbelpore,
With tired legs and feet so sore,
He's staggered, sailed, rode and ran,
All round the world and back again.

MAUDE *has reached the other side and hugs* JAN.
JAN *hops on* MAUDE's *back and she wades in, transporting him back towards* TING TANG.

MAUDE: There's bin plenty sightins of y'over the years, Jan.

JAN: I bet there ave.

MAUDE: Lisha Ball said a man down Par said e saw you rowin a tuck boat for a seine net company.

JAN: Did did e?

MAUDE: That was eighteen-eight. Lisha Ball said there was a man down Indian Queens told im you was married and sold your wife at Summercourt Fair for four shillin! E said you bought a pig!

JAN: Hah!

MAUDE: I said that id'n like Jan to do a thing like that, e never liked pig!

JAN: Hell! See that trout?

MAUDE: Hold still! I did not! Then last year, eighteen-fourteen, Perrantide or Midsummer? Father was ome anyhow, Lisha Ball come round t'elp your father sink the well and I said g'day Lisha, any sightins? E said ab'm you eard? I said what, e said Jan's dead! Your son's dead!

JAN: Hah!

MAUDE: I said e id'n dead!

JAN: How did I die?

MAUDE: I said now you listen ere Lisha Ball! I said boy Jan's runned off and we ab'm seed'n for nine year but that dun't mean e's dead! Dun't mean e's come to any harm whatsoever! Christ boy you'm some weight . . . I said boy Jan's too full of 'is own pride, too important to imself, to die young. I said e's too damn pigheaded Lisha Ball! I said e's safe inside some big house eatin butchers meat and tellin lies. Bugger id'n dead!

JAN: I arn't dead.

MAUDE: We eld a service for e anyhow, just in case. Service of Remembrance. Just in case you *ad* died. Can't recall oo twas oo, Primitive Methodists or Bible Christians, aw I think twas the Thumpers, cus Betty Elder's third 'usband, 'arry, e got converted and runned off. Joined the circuit, preaching. She never forgived you for that, Betty Elder. Jan you've grawed big as a bullock!

JAN: Bin eatin good butcher's meat, Mother.

MAUDE: Where've e bin anyhow?

JAN: Bin round the world, Mother.

MAUDE: Took e nine years? World id'n that big boy.

They are close to the opposite bank of the river.

JAN: I stopped off ere and there. And I was shipwrecked three times.

MAUDE: WHAT?! You was SHIPWRECKED?!

MAUDE *drops* JAN *in the river.*

JAN: Aww, Mother!

MAUDE: You was shipwrecked? And y'ask me to carry y'across the damn river?!

JAN *is drenched but he's managed to keep his carpet bag dry.*

JAN: Look at this! Look at it! Look at that! Aw Mother! My best blasted rigout! Ruined! Thass my best suit! My biggest hat! Look at it! Soaked! Colour's runnin, look at it!

MAUDE *is sitting on the river bank, replacing her footwear.*

MAUDE: I suppose you wish to eat with us tonight.

JAN: My best damned rigout!

MAUDE: We got your grandmother still with us, your brother Colan's blind, your three sisters . . .

JAN: Three?

MAUDE: How many do e want?

JAN: Didn't ave any when I left.

MAUDE: They're out nestin, your father and brother Arthur's down bal workin doublers, I got food for four to feed ten then you show up out the blue.

JAN: I'll buy some butcher's meat.

MAUDE: You'll buy nothin! I got plenty ome without your charity.

MAUDE *and* JAN *have left the river behind,* MAUDE *striding out ahead with* JAN *waddling behind, arms and legs akimbo, he suffers extreme discomfort with his wet clothes. He holds his bag at arm's length.* ANN ROSCROW *approaches* MAUDE *from the opposite direction and* MAUDE *hails her.*

MAUDE: Oo! Mrs Roscrow! How's business?

JAN *arrives on the scene, legs wide apart, arms out. He spies* ROSCROW *and his jaw drops with infatuation.* ROSCROW *stares at* JAN *with disbelief.*

ROSCROW: Who's this?

MAUDE: My son Mrs Roscrow. Jan. E falled in the river.

JAN: I bin round the world.

ROSCROW: Good grief!

ROSCROW *wanders off, dumbstruck.*

JAN: Who was that?

MAUDE: Ann Roscrow. Er usband went to Jesus and left er oldin the fort.

JAN: Up Ting Tang?

MAUDE: Principal adventurer she is, shrewd as a cat. She once belonged to the Only the Sober Circle of Women but it was rumoured she elped er husband on 'is way to the hereafter so she left them after that . . .

JAN: Did you see the way she looked at me Mother? Did you see? Love! Love at first sight! In all the miles I've travelled round the world I've never set eyes on a woman half as beautiful as that. And she loves me!

MAUDE: There's a sinew of opinion, what ripple through the Tent Methodists, that she'm a witch . . .

JAN *is looking off down the road towards* ROSCROW.

JAN: Where does she live? How can I meet her?

MAUDE: Now the Bible Christians reckon she's a man dressed up as a woman and quote as proof the lack of children . . .

JAN: No children? Joy! Joy!

MAUDE: The Calvinists say tis er divine right to adventure in mines, and if er usband's gone before she'll more'n likely foller . . .

JAN: Imagine Mother, with your clothes all wet, clinging to your body, walking with your legs apart and your suit hangin heavy! Are these the conditions under which one falls in love?

MAUDE: I'd oped you might've altered in the last nine years Jan . . .

JAN: And she loves me!

MAUDE: . . . grown wiser.

JAN *and* MAUDE *have reached the top of the hill overlooking* TING TANG *village. They look down on the scene below them.* TREFUSIS *sings a triumphal anthem to* JAN's *homecoming.*

ANTHEM

Jan May! Travellor! Son of Ting Tang!
None the wiser! Weary! And wet!
World-wandered, love struck man!
Welcome home! Welcome home! Well
met!

BETTY ELDER *washes her linen in the
stream,* GRAN *sits outside the* MAY*'s
house, with* COLAN, JAN*'s blind
brother, at her feet.* MAUDE *emits a
blood curdling yell.*

MAUDE: Look ere, look! Look look oo's
ome!Look! E's back!

MAUDE *rushes down into the village and*
JAN *follows after.* BETTY ELDER
looks up from the stream, GRAN *and*
COLAN *don't show much interest.*

MAUDE: Look! Look! E's back!

The sight of JAN *in familiar surroundings
is too much for her and she flings her arms
around him and hugs him, sobbing.*

GRAN: What the hell a you got on boy?

JAN: Tis soakin wet, Gran.

COLAN: What e got on, Gran?

GRAN: Three or four carpets.

BETTY ELDER *shouts from the river.*

BETTY: You're supposed to be dead!

JAN: Ullo Betty!

BETTY: We eld a service for you! Send
y'on your way!

MAUDE *releases* JAN *and shows him off
to the others.*

JAN: Colan, lost your eyes?

COLAN: Lost em blastin.

GRAN: Short fuse.

COLAN: No I was tampin.

GRAN: Rammin it ome too tight.

COLAN: Twas a spark, from the bar, iron
bar.

GRAN: Too bloody lazy.

COLAN: Christ in hell twas a spark, went
up in me face!

JAN: Sorry to hear that, Colan.

GRAN: Where've e bin?

JAN: Bin round the world, Gran.

GRAN: Go Paraguay?

JAN: Paraguay? Oh yes.

GRAN: Didya run into Dasher Smeely?

JAN: No I didn't. Just missed'n.

GRAN: Bugger owe me money. Look'n out
when you get back.

A distant bell sounds.

MAUDE: There! Thass the end a core and I
ab'm thought about food!

MAUDE *runs into the house.* BETTY
ELDER *approaches* JAN.

BETTY: We eld a service for you! You're
supposed to be dead! You're responsible
for a conversion!

She pinches JAN *hard.*

JAN: Ouch! What the hell was that for?!

BETTY: I arn't convinced.

GRAN: She lost er usband cus a you.

BETTY: E defied conversion. E was
staunch against em all. Then we ad your
memorial service, up Pasco Walters'
barn . . .

GRAN: No. Under a tree it was . . .

BETTY: Twas a thumper wannit? Preacher
oo come round? Thumper.

COLAN: Jumper.

GRAN: Shaker.

BETTY (*calls inside*): Maude! You was a
thumper then wanne?!

MAUDE (*inside*): When?!

BETTY: When boy Jan died!

MAUDE: (*inside*): I left em after that!

BETTY: Thumper. They're the worse of
the lot.

GRAN: Thump thump thump!

BETTY (*to* GRAN): You dropped! (*to*
JAN, *indicating* GRAN.) She dropped!
Dropped straight to er knees, soon as she
got there! Straight to er knees . . .

GRAN: I always drop. They dun't bother
with e then. There's undreds claimed me
for Jesus – Lutherans, Calvins,
Primitives, Romans, drop straight to your
knees at the lot and they think you'm one
a them, but you gotta stay down. They get
ya if ya git up.

BETTY: Harry dropped, then e got up . . .

JAN (*to* COLAN): I thought er first usband was 'arry . . .

COLAN: They was all called 'arry . . .

GRAN: See?

BETTY: All the while matey in the pulpit . . .

GRAN: Under a tree it was . . .

COLAN: Hot. June Month . . .

BETTY: His eyes was bulgin . . .

COLAN: Whose?

GRAN: Not yours . . .

BETTY: E ad a luscious way a talking . . .

COLAN (*imitating preacher*): Now then brethren, I'm gonna tell e a li'll bit 'safternoon 'bout eb'm!

GRAN: . . . And a beard . . .

COLAN: Heaven! Damme to Christ almighty in hellfire what do a crowda miserable sinners from Ting Tang knaw 'bout eb'm!

BETTY: I knew Harry was gone when e got up off 'is knees and went up front, swayin . . .

GRAN: E should never a got up!

COLAN: Let's ask Abram! Abram bin up in eaven a brave while! (*Turns his face skywards and yells.*) ABRAM!

BETTY: E was callin, swoonin, big man see, e ad tears streaming down is face, I was up the back there screamin 'Arry! Come back! Come back!

COLAN: What sorta place is eb'm! Tell we down ere 'bout eb'm wille! (*Affecting a deep voice, looking down.*) Gloree upon glorees son! (*Looking up.*) That so? That so is a? I thought as much but these are hellborn savages wouldn' believe it!

BETTY: E shoulda stayed where e was when e dropped!

GRAN: She was there . . . screamin at im . . .

BETTY: Arry! Arry! Come back ere! For e lays ands on ya!

COLAN: Come down! Thou great Jehovah! Bring thy stone ammer with e

and scat the hard hearts of these wicked and perverse people! . . .

GRAN: I said to'n, 'fore e got up, face flat in the dust, mouth fulla daisies, I said stick ere Arry. Dun't let the bugger git old a ya!

COLAN: . . . Oh grave! Where is thy victory! The day of vengeance is in my heart! Enter! Enter into the holiest! By the new and living way! Let the chains fall off your tongues!

BETTY: There was people stickin y'in the ribs, pokin about with their fingers . . .

COLAN: Gimme Christ or else I die!

BETTY: Tearing the bark off trees . . .

GRAN: Twas a sad day Betty . . .

COLAN: Acquaint! Acquaint thyself with im and be at peace!

BETTY: Then e went . . .

GRAN: Like a lamb in a trance . . .

COLAN: Come out!! And let Sodom feel its doom!

BETTY (*in tears*): Didn' say goodbye or nothin . . .

COLAN: Thou lewdly revellest in the bowels of God!

GRAN: Not a word. Not to any of us . . .

COLAN: Where now is Lot!

BETTY: Preacher chap got down off the pulpit . . .

GRAN: Tree it was . . .

COLAN: At Zoar safe! Where is his wife! Salt for pilchards!

BETTY: Took 'Arry by the hand . . . and . . . and . . .

COLAN: Great Og and Agog! Where are e!

BETTY: Led im away into the yonder . . .

GRAN: E's preachin imself now, under a tree.

COLAN: Followin Christ!

BETTY: All cus a you!

BETTY *runs off in tears.* MAUDE *emerges from the house.*

MAUDE: Jan, you want flesh or fish?

JAN: 'Sorta fish?

MAUDE: Pilcher. Flesh is mutton . . .

JAN: Hah! Pilchard!

MAUDE *goes indoors.*

GRAN: She's bin savin it up for ya, for when you returned.

JAN: Ave a?

GRAN: Nine years she's ad that pilchard.

JAN (*calling indoors*): I'll ave the flesh!

The MEN *approach from the mine. A stream of tired miners, including* TOM, LISHA *and* ARTHUR, *enter the village and make their way to their homes.* MAUDE *runs out with a plate of mutton for* JAN, *and scuttles back indoors.* GRAN *moves* COLAN *out of the way to make way for* TOM *and* ARTHUR, *who sit in chairs provided by* GRAN. *They are too tired to notice* JAN. MAUDE *emerges with a bowl of mutton broth.* TOM *and* ARTHUR *put their heads back and open their mouths,* MAUDE *spoonfeeds them the broth. They are too tired to feed themselves.*

JAN: Ullo Father.

GRAN: Dun't disturb im while e's eating.

COLAN: Bin working doublers.

JAN: Ah.

GRAN: They gotta rich lode down bal.

COLAN: Great North Lode. Go bal six in the morning, come ome six at night.

While TOM *and* ARTHUR *are being fed,* JAN *sits beside* COLAN.

JAN: What do you do with yourself all day, Colan?

COLAN: Aw, sell sand, buy bones . . .

GRAN: When e can get it . . .

COLAN: I take ole donkey down, ole, moyle, itch er up to the cart . . .

GRAN: When the wheel dun't drop off . . .

COLAN: Git the girls to lead me down there, down beach . . .

GRAN: When they id'n raidin nests . . .

COLAN: Thass nestin time Gran . . . Git the ole shovel . . .

GRAN: When the ilt id'n split . . .

COLAN: Dig up the sand . . .

GRAN: If the tide appen to be out . . .

COLAN: Load up the cart, and start knockin on doors.

GRAN: When there's anyone ome.

COLAN: I dun't get round to it that often.

GRAN: When alligators swim in Mevagissey Bay.

COLAN: There's too many snags reely . . .

MAUDE *has finished feeding* TOM *and* ARTHUR, *who are now asleep.*

MAUDE: Thomas. Tom. Wake up! See oo's ere! Tom!

TOM *wakes up.*

TOM: Whass for dinner?

MAUDE: You've ad your dinner!

TOM: What was it?

MAUDE: Boy Jan's back!

TOM: Jan?

MAUDE: Your long lost son! Jan!

TOM: Jan!

JAN: Ullo Father . . .

TOM: Christ boy thass some outfit you got on . . .

GRAN: Bal shag . . .

JAN: Tis soakin wet.

TOM: Where've e bin?

JAN: In the river.

TOM: In the river? Ear that Mother? Boy's bin in the river. What, on a boat in the river? Which river?

JAN: Mother dropped me in the river. Me suit's soaked. I bin round the world!

TOM: What e drop'n in the river for Maude?

MAUDE: Cus e was shipwrecked!

MAUDE *has piled up the dishes and is walking towards the stream.* LISHA BALL *runs up.*

LISHA: Maude! Maude!

MAUDE: Ullo Lisha . . .

LISHA: Ear 'bout Jan?

MAUDE: What?

LISHA: E's dead now!

MAUDE: Is a?

LISHA: E got et be alligator in Paraguay.

MAUDE: Dear o dear.

LISHA: E'd bin round the world and e
    falled in a river they got out there and a
    big 'gator swimmed up and swallered 'n
    ole! E was sufferin discomfort before 'is
    death on account e'd ad nothin to eat but
    monkey flesh and soft fruit so tis best all
    round. Tis all over the parish,
    poor chap . . .

JAN: What?!

MAUDE: Jan wouldn' get isself et be
    alligator!

LISHA: E wouldn' ave no say in the
    matter . . .

GRAN: E'd talk im out of it.

JAN: Crikey!

LISHA (*indicates* JAN): Oo's this?

MAUDE: That's Jan

LISHA *is suspicious. He studies* JAN *and
    his suit.*

LISHA (*to* MAUDE): You sure?

MAUDE: I'm 'is mother

LISHA (*to* JAN): Whass your name?

JAN: Jan!

LISHA: Where d'y get this suit?

JAN: Er, someplace, I forget.

LISHA: Plymouth?

MAUDE: E's bin round the world Lisha . . .

LISHA: It's wet.

TOM: E was shipwrecked.

LISHA: I seen this outfit before.

JAN: Where?

LISHA: Someplace. I forget.

JAN: Well ah, there's plenty more like it.

ALL (*disbelief*): Is there?

JAN: Oh, practically everywhere you go in
    the world every other man is wearing a
    suit identical to this . . .

LISHA: You buy it off a Frenchman?

JAN: Yes. Yes.

LISHA *sees* BETTY *emerge from her
    house.*

LISHA: Ah! Betty!

BETTY: What?

LISHA: There's bin a sighting of your
    beloved! E was last seen up Bugle with a
    bottle a gin in 'is 'and recitin to a flock a
    sheep 'bout the life ereafter . . .

BETTY: Hah! What was 'is text?

LISHA: Summin 'bout the wicked gettin
    their just deserts. Gin bottle was half
    empty . . .

LISHA *goes.*

BETTY (*to* JAN): I ope your satisfied with
    that!

She goes.

JAN: Christ in hellfire tis like I never bin
    away!

MAUDE: Oh we're all delighted you're
    back, arn't we Thomas? Arthur?

TOM: Arthur's still asleep.

GRAN: Leave im be.

JAN *removes a selection of dry clothes
    from his bag. The clothes are just as gaudy
    as the ones he has on. He places the clothes
    in a pile on the bench, then tips the
    remaining contents of the bag out onto the
    ground before him.* TEN THOUSAND
    POUNDS *in all denominations, notes,
    bonds, spill from the bag into a crisp,
    gleaming pile before his family, who watch
    silently whilst he does this. He leaves the
    money for them to ponder, and he changes
    into his dry clothes as he speaks:*

JAN: That's what the world had to offer me.
    To you, maybe, it look a fortune, but tis
    no more'n dust to my pocket. Cus the
    world's a brother to me now. I can stray
    out there and cross continents with ease.
    I've traversed whole countries without
    ever knowing I bin in em. I bin to places
    where they d'grow people to fit the mines
    and paint em black to save washing. I've
    spoke with men whose language I could
    never understand. Argued with princes,
    and popes. They tole me they was popes
    in a language I could never understand
    but who am I to question that? I debated
    with em and eld me ground, gambled with
    em and took their cash. Flirted with their
    mistresses! My Christ, Mother, what a

vast and various herd is the human species
and I tackled em all. I'm tired of
adventure now. I've come ome to rest and
share the fruits of my endeavour. Oh yes.
Take it. Take it all. Do, take it.

Nobody moves.

COLAN (*quietly, to* GRAN): What is it?

GRAN: Nothin much.

JAN: Ten? Fifteen? Twenty thousand
pounds, I havn't bothered to count it.
Notes, coins, deeds, dollars, francs,
pesetas, pounds. Tis all yours . . .

*Nobody moves. ARTHUR is still asleep
with his head flung back, mouth open, and
snoring.*

MAUDE: Shall I wake Arthur, Jan? See if e
want some?

JAN: Aw Mother dear sweet Mother, bless
you no there's no need for that . . . it id'n
goin nowhere. If you're too proud to take
it Father, remember I'm your son too and
I earned it just as hard as if I'd sweat down
bal. Is it too much to comprehend? I can
understand that. Think of it as a door,
Father. A door that's opened, and you
can walk through that door. And on the
other side is the garden of Eden. Full of
apples. Thass all it is, Father. A door.
Tidn' money, tis a door! A plain old oak
wood door. With perhaps a big house in
the grounds of this ere garden of Eden,
Father, with exotic trees and peacocks!

MAUDE: Oh, peacocks . . .

JAN: Or has the fear of God and the dread
of mamon bin etched too deep in ya, by
the Only the Sobers, the Methodists, the
Enthusiasts, the Thumpers, Mother, who
say tis no-one's right but theirs to taste the
riches of this life and the poor will suffer
til they die and fly to heaven? Well I telle I
bin all round the bastard world and
there's not one dead man I've met who's
happy! There's no such thing as the life
hereafter, you gotta take what you can in
this! I didn't cross the Gobi desert on
faith, Mother! I ired a camel! Thass the
way the world go round!

MAUDE: Will you let your father go bed
now Jan? E gotta core to work at six . . .

JAN: Don't you want it? Whass the matter
with you all! Don't you want it? I'm giving
it to ya!

TOM *rises and slowly walks indoors.* JAN
shouts after him:

JAN: I couldn' come ome wi' nothin
could I!

GRAN: Why the hell not boy? If you
couldn' come back wi' nothin, why come
back at all?

COLAN *rises and takes* GRAN's *hand.*

GRAN: If you've bin dinin on fumigoes
with the mightiest dons in Spain I
wouldna thought this little lot woulda
lasted ya more'n a week.

GRAN *leads* COLAN *indoors.* JAN,
MAUDE *and* ARTHUR, *who is still
asleep, remain.* JAN *is now changed into
his dry clothes, which are even more
preposterous than before. He folds his wet
clothes and replaces them and his money
in the carpet bag.*

MAUDE: See Father's got a sturt on now,
with this great North Lode. E bin workin
doublers with Arthur. I run a tight ship,
we got no credit nowhere and we
managed to save up thirty-seven shillin.
Soon as e come off doublers Father's
gonna cut some stone and build on two
more rooms and a linney . . .

JAN: A linney!

MAUDE: We're gonna clear out the back,
make room for a pig. And after that, your
father ope to gain the post of Captain at
Bal. And the girls a soon be big enough
to work the bellows and break ore, so you
see boy, I think we dun't altogether need
it.

JAN's *bag is packed.*

JAN: Goodbye Mother.

MAUDE (*tearful*): Goodbye boy . . .

JAN: Where's the nearest Inn, Brigan?

MAUDE: Oh Jan, walk past Brigan.
They're wicked people up Brigan, they
tear the limbs off Ting Tang people and
eat granite in their pies. Walk past Brigan
. . .

JAN: I've bin round the world, Mother!
Brigan wun't old no surprises for me!
Brigan's five miles up the road!

JAN *starts to go.*

MAUDE: You'll come back one day . . .

JAN: One day, yeah.

JAN goes. MAUDE wakes ARTHUR.

MAUDE: Arthur. Come on son, wake up . . .

ARTHUR wakes from a deep sleep and stretches.

ARTHUR: Gaw Christ. Mother I can't go on with this. Bastard doublers. How does Father do it? Near forty-four year old and ere am I, nineteen and half, dead with fatigue! What did I ave for me supper I dunno what I ad for me supper ad summin for me supper must ave . . .

MAUDE: Mutton broth.

ARTHUR: Mutton broth. Tis a poor life when a man can't enjoy 'is food, tis no life at all when e can't remember what e ad. Did I hear shoutin?

MAUDE: When?

ARTHUR: In me sleep.

MAUDE: Coulda bin Jan.

ARTHUR: Jan? Brother Jan?

MAUDE: E was ere.

ARTHUR: As e gone?

MAUDE: Yes, dear. E's bin and gone.

ARTHUR: And I missed'n?

MAUDE: You was asleep.

ARTHUR: Did no bugger think to wake me up?

MAUDE: It was discussed and Jan particularly said to leave you sleep.

ARTHUR: Why?!

MAUDE: I don't know boy, I don't know. If you want the answer to that one you must ask Jan . . .

ARTHUR: E id'n ere!

MAUDE: Then I shouldn' bother with it.

MAUDE has started to head for the house.

ARTHUR: 'As e altered much?

MAUDE: 'Ardly at all.

ARTHUR: Whass e bin up to?

MAUDE: Oh, e ad argument with a pope . . .

ARTHUR: With a pope?

MAUDE: And I dropped im in the river . . .

ARTHUR: Where's e gone to?

MAUDE: Brigan.

ARTHUR: Brigan? Brigan!

He follows MAUDE indoors.
TREFUSIS enters and sings a song.

TREFUSIS: Jan May, son of Ting Tang,
Returned a wealthy man.
They welcomed him as best they could,
And now he's gone again.

Jan May, in golden jacket,
Laid the contents of his pocket
Out before them. That was good.
But they turned their backs upon it.

Jan May has gone to Brigan.
There he'll find a welcome.
Our enemy will treat him like a god.
He'll not come here again.

GONETTA BATE *sits at a table in the*
PICK *and* GAD INN, BRIGAN.
SALATHIEL TRENANNIGAN *stands*
with her back to GONETTA, *leaning on the*
bar, drinking a mug of gin.

GONETTA: This ere is the Pick and Gad Inn, Brigan. Tis a pest 'ole. We're open but you wouldn' know it. She frightened em off. (*Indicates* SALATHIEL.) She achieved in one proclamation what the Only the Sober Circle a Women failed to do in a decade. She stopped Brigan drinkin.

SALATHIEL *slams down her mug on the*
bar and turns towards GONETTA. *She*
walks across the room and stands over her.
She is a large, predatory woman dressed as
a man in clawhammer coat, stovepipe hat
and hobnailed boots. She sports a
moustache. Her waistcoat just meets
across her belly, which she thrusts at
GONETTA.

SALATHIEL: Tell me the time, Gonetta.

GONETTA *takes a watch from*
SALATHIEL's *waistcoat pocket and*
reads off the time:

GONETTA: Nine o'clock.

SALATHIEL: Where's all the custom?

GONETTA: Ome.

SALATHIEL: Not drinkin? Thass unlike em!

GONETTA: They got no money, with the mine shut.

SALATHIEL: It id'n their money I'm askin for my gin Gonetta.

GONETTA: No. Tis their bodies.

SALATHIEL: It seemed a watertight enough scheme to me, Gonetta, when I dreamed it up. I shut down Brigan Bal, deprive the male population of its income. The younger men can no longer pay cash for their gin so I advertise terms contiguous to flesh! To the married men of course I offer credit, but married men seldom drink and single men, sadly, appear not to have took up the gauntlet. How do you account for this sorry lack of passion, Gonetta? Is it my demeanour? My bearin? My conduct? My mien?

GONETTA: I'd say twas your suit.

SALATHIEL: My suit!

GONETTA: Tis ardly conducive to romance.

SALATHIEL: And I say you should never judge a man by the way e dress, cus there's always the chance there might be a passionate woman underneath. Sadly God has gived me men's work to do on his fair earth and this suit to do it in. God send me eccentric custom, Gonetta, or we die starvin and celibate . . .

GONETTA: Well it might just be that somewhere on this earth there's somebody who God in all his wisdom has dressed as daft as you, but I doubt it.

There is a loud knock at the door.

SALATHIEL: Ah! Who could this be?! Young Kenal? His brother Raw? Kay Bray's son Kitto? All of em perhaps? See to the door Gonetta!

GONETTA *opens the door and* JAN *enters, dressed in his outrageous clothes and carrying his bag.* GONETTA *takes one look at him and turns her eyes to heaven. Then she shuts and locks the door.* SALATHIEL *and* JAN *look each other up and down.*

SALATHIEL: Thass a damn fine suit sir.

JAN: Thank you.

SALATHIEL: Damn fine. Where was that suit ah, assembled? I can't say knit, for that would denigrate the fine cut a the cloth. I can't say sewn together, for the same could be said of a sack. And in truth sir the suit you carry 'pon your broad back owe its predigree more to a Boulton and Watt precision steam pumpin engine than shall we say a sack! No sir there's suits worn today that if you filled em fulla barley and stood em in a line you couldn' tell they wad'n sacks. And I dare venture to observe if e took this suit along the butcher e a make a pretty profit from the top grade meat e found inside . . .

JAN: Meat?

GONETTA *prods* JAN's *body.*

GONETTA: Tis good'n ard.

SALATHIEL *smiles.*

SALATHIEL: So. Where d'e get this suit thun?

JAN: I forget. I bin round the world. I travelled all over.

SALATHIEL: A capital city. Thass a capital city suit sir. Rome. Madrid. St. Petersburg. Sorta suit Mr Napoleon Bonaparte would be appy to be seen dead in. Christ in hell thass some suit.

JAN: I could say you was somewhat strikingly dressed yourself.

SALATHIEL: Thank you sir. Oh thank you. But yourself sir, who is he that cometh from Edom, dressed in the dyed fabrics of Bozrah?

JAN: My name is Jan May and I wish to purchase a room for the night.

SALATHIEL *offers* JAN *her hand by way of introduction.*

SALATHIEL: Salathiel Trenannigan.

JAN: Christ in hell, thass a man's name!

SALATHIEL: I do a man's job. I bin a kibble-lander years back. I own Brigan Mine now. Sure as hell own it. No sir, wouldn' old for me to go be a name like Grace Briney.

JAN: You own Brigan Mine?

SALATHIEL: Yes sir. She's knacked, for want of capital. But what of that? I still got the Inn. No there's one area where I differ from a man and thass passion. And I'll tell e whass up with the world today and you'll bear me out, bein round it, and thass there's no passion left. Tis all enthusiasm. Now I can work up enthusiasm 'long with the rest of em, but I d'back it up wi' passion. Take your fine suit sir. I've showed not a little enthusiasm for that suit tonight sir, no?

JAN (*uncertain*): Yes?

SALATHIEL: But there's bin little rats nibblin away inside that first-class brain of yours posin the question where's the passion? Where's the passion in this woman? And runnin alongside that there li'l question, trying ard to keep up, is the posture why, at half past nine at night, with a knacked bal in the neighbourhood and a legion of idle men, is this Inn empty?

JAN: It er, ad crossed my mind, yes.

SALATHIEL: Come sir, you've travelled round the world from Akaba to Tregadillet, and there ab'm bin one Inn empty at alf past nine at night . . . and the answer to that one is plain as a bullock's tongue. They got less stomick for *passion* these boys than they ave for cheap gin! Now thun. You wanna bed for tonight.

JAN: Er, well . . .

SALATHIEL: Man who's travelled round the world you've shared berths wi' bigger men than me and I ave the softest flesh. My when I hit the duckdown I can do a woman's job. (*Fingers his jacket.*) I'll pick the cloth off your back delicate.

JAN: But I'm in love! I can't break a vow of fidelity . . .

SALATHIEL: Tid'n love I'm asking of ya, tis passion . . .

GONETTA: E's bin took be the methodists.

JAN: I got no fear of the afterlife!

GONETTA: Got too much fear in this.

JAN: I'm my own man!

SALATHIEL: No! You're lookin at me and the passion's wellin up inside ya. But your fine suit and clean face speak to me and say I'm a man, Salathiel, who has an appearance in this world, all of it, being

round it, which I wish my fellow men to take note of and respect. And that appearance, in spite of the passion I feel for this woman, does not encompass kissin a lady who wear for example, a moustache upon er upper lip!

JAN: Yes! You hit upon the truth there!

SALATHIEL: Then I'll take if off!

SALATHIEL *removes her moustache. She stands back.*

JAN: Tis somewhat more'n the moustache.

SALATHIEL (*removing her clothes*): The stovepipe hat? The clawhammer coat? The hobnailed boots?

SALATHIEL *is soon down to her undergarments.*

JAN: No! No!

JAN *looks round him. There's no escape.* GONETTA *guards the door with a pick handle.* JAN *drops to his knees and prays.*

JAN: Oh God!

GONETTA: E's on *our* side.

JAN *spills the contents of his bag across the floor.* SALATHIEL *and* GONETTA *stare in disbelief at his riches.*

JAN: What's this Brigan bal? I'll buy if off ya.

SALATHIEL: Did I mention I was sellin?

JAN: You said it was knacked.

SALATHIEL: Knacked sir? No sir. There's enough copper under Brigan to plate the whole of France. But tis best left under, till the price get yeasty. On the other 'and, for a man a means, for a capital city man with money to burn, you could afford to send an army down there and raise a thousand tons in one big dollop, flood the market and destroy the competition. After that the price is yours. Yes sir, for a man of means it got potential.

JAN: Well I'm nothin if not a man of means, and if you give me a single room for the night with a lock on the door I'll buy it off ya.

SALATHIEL: Let's hear an offer.

JAN: Shall we say five hundred?

SALATHIEL: Five hundred what?

JAN: Five undred pound.

SALATHIEL: That's without the pumpin engine.

JAN: Eh?

SALATHIEL: You dun't need no pumpin engine. Best off without a pumpin engine.

GONETTA *furnishes* JAN *with a mug of gin and tobacco.*

JAN: How much did we say?

SALATHIEL: Seven hundred.

JAN: Will you take it in pesetas?

SALATHIEL: I'll take it in manure.

JAN: Thass two thousand pesetas, nearlybout.

SALATHIEL: Give us three and I'll throw in the pumpin engine.

JAN: Three with the pumpin engine.

SALATHIEL: Did I say three?

JAN: Three what?

SALATHIEL: Three thousand pound.

JAN: Three thousand pound?

SALATHIEL: Thass too much don't you think?

JAN: It's a bloody fortune!

SALATHIEL: I quite agree. We'll say four thousand.

JAN: Pounds?

SALATHIEL: Pesetas.

JAN: Thass near a thousand pound!

SALATHIEL: Thass more like it. Three's far too much.

JAN: Four thousand pesetas.

SALATHIEL: Thass without the pumpin engine.

JAN: With*out* the pumpin engine?

SALATHIEL: You want the pumpin engine?

JAN: For four thousands I *get* the pumpin engine!

SALATHIEL: That was three thousand pound you got the pumpin engine but we agreed three was too much.

JAN: We certainly did.

SALATHIEL: Than I'll drop to two with the pumpin engine.

JAN: Pesetas?

SALATHIEL: Pounds.

JAN: Two thousand pound?!

SALATHIEL: Thank you sir, that sound reasonable.

SALATHIEL *shakes* JAN *by the hand.*

JAN: With the pumpin engine.

SALATHIEL: Thass ten thousand pesetas.

JAN *starts to count out ten thousand pesetas.*

SALATHIEL: You didn' come by this lot sinkin wells.

JAN: I did not.

SALATHIEL: Well I arn't surprised you're a wealthy man with a business head like yours . . .

JAN: You think so?

SALATHIEL: My Christ Almighty tis twenty years since I struck a bargain like that one.

JAN: You're lookin at a man who's bankrupted sultans.

SALATHIEL: I arn't at all surprised.

JAN: And I got the pumpin engine!

GONETTA: I ope so.

JAN: Uh?

SALATHIEL *paces the floor.*

SALATHIEL: Y'know that was a capital city deal you struck there. I'm no capital city man Mr May, why you'd stretch my memory to the backa beyond if you was to ask me the last time I crossed the parish boundary. Forgive me. I rode to Plymouth a fortnight ago to see off Boney. But Plymouth? 'Ardly Madagascar! And before that? Doomsday! But often a knowledge of local affairs in business will take you a long way further in the world than shall we say intimacy with the value of the drachma against the Dutch noble . . .

JAN: Oh I'm intimate with that . . .

SALATHIEL: I thought you might be. On the other 'and, locally, a man with that kinda capital city knowledge on the tip of 'is tongue would cut a great deal of trust and admiration. Particularly amongst farmers.

JAN: Ah . . .

GONETTA: But which farmers?

SALATHIEL: Which, rich, farmers?

GONETTA: That require a knowledge altogether local.

SALATHIEL: Intimate.

JAN: There. Twelve thousand pesetas.

SALATHIEL *reaches into her bosom and withdraws a battered parchment.*

SALATHIEL: And here we have the deed.

JAN: Good. Now thun. My room.

JAN *takes the deed and places it in his bag. He scoops the remainder of the money into the bag and slings it across his shoulder.*

SALATHIEL: Mr May, you're a mineowner now.

JAN: Jan May. Mineowner. God in heaven.

GONETTA: She can do better than that, Mr May . . .

JAN: Oh?

GONETTA: You've yet to talk of banks . . .

JAN: She owns a bank?

SALATHIEL: Thought of ownin a bank quicken the blood?

JAN: Christ in hell it got it pumpin bloody fast . . .

GONETTA: Jan May. Mineowner . . . Banker!

JAN: Banker! How could we go about it? Buying a bank?

SALATHIEL: Oh thass pillow talk that is. I do all my bank business orizontal . . .

JAN: Jesus Christ! Jesus Christ in hellfire!

SALATHIEL *opens her arms to* JAN. JAN *drops his bag and leaps into* SALATHIEL's *arms.* GONETTA's *song, optional:*

GONETTA: I watched em through a crack in the floor,
I saw it with me own damned eyes.
When he flagged and drooped and she wanted more,
When the iron drained from 'is thighs,

One little word revived im
BANKER
One hot breath in his ear
BANKER
That parodym got em pumpin,
BANKER
Cranked im into gear!

They was at it through til the crowing cock,
Dawn couldn't quench their fire,
Like two wild pigs in an empty sack,
Each coupled to the other's desire.

A loud knock on the door. GONETTA *opens the door and* HAILSHAM *enters.* GONETTA *gestures skywards.*

GONETTA: E bought the mine off er last night.

HAILSHAM: E's a braver man than me.

GONETTA: She clinched the deal with talk of banks. Never fail.

HAILSHAM: What plan does he have for the mine?

GONETTA: I'm quite sure e dosn't have a plan in 'is head, Mr Hailsham.

HAILSHAM: You think not?

GONETTA: E's gotta bag fulla money and a head fulla dreams.

SALATHIEL *enters. She is brisk and businesslike.*

SALATHIEL: Aha! Mr Hailsham! Good morning Mr Hailsham! Welcome back!

HAILSHAM: Good morning Mr Trenannigan.

JAN *enters. He is the antithesis of* SALATHIEL *half-dressed, disorientated and shagged-out.* SALATHIEL *presides over introductions:*

SALATHIEL: Mr Hailsham, Mr May. Mr May. Mr Hailsham.

JAN: How do you do sir . . .

HAILSHAM: And you Mr May . . .

SALATHIEL: Gonetta! Gin and fat cigars!

GONETTA: I can't abide an early mornin rush.

SALATHIEL: How's the market?

HAILSHAM: Tin's up, copper's static, lead's soft.

JAN: I'm relieved to hear that.

HAILSHAM: Slate's edgey, granite's bottomed.

SALATHIEL: Kumpfernickel?

HAILSHAM: Firm.

SALATHIEL: Sounds volatile.

HAILSHAM: I don't like the look of it.

SALATHIEL: It's those damned Bolivians again.

GONETTA *slams à flagon of gin, a box of cigars and three glasses on the table. She takes the cigars and hands them round.*

SALATHIEL: Gentlemen. Let us sit and talk of banks.

SALATHIEL *sits and leans back in her chair.* HAILSHAM *and* JAN *do likewise.* GONETTA *lights their cigars and they puff on them in a satisfied way.* GONETTA *speaks to the audience.*

GONETTA: Bloody remarkable what a cigar does for 'em. Rolled up mass of stinkin weed, transports em to the golden palace of the Raj.

JAN: We should, we should open up a bank.

HAILSHAM: That's a proposal of vision if I may say, sir.

JAN: Thank you Mr Hailsham. Thanks sir.

HAILSHAM: Shows a deep understanding of the market.

JAN: Well, see, I've bin to Bolivia.

HAILSHAM: You have?

JAN: Oh all over Europe . . .

SALATHIEL: We wanna no-nonsense, big-deposit bank, such as farmers favour.

JAN: A capital city bank.

HAILSHAM: A bank where they'd 'bring their cash in cartloads, and lodge it there to rot.

SALATHIEL: Naturally Mr May will be the President of this bank . . .

JAN: President . . .

SALATHIEL: The figurehead. Havin been out a country for the last nine years, with his capital city wardrobe and European airs, he's exactly the sorta chap who'd

command great authority in Truro, with farmers . . .

JAN: This is music to my ears . . .

HAILSHAM: Do we have sufficient cash to start this bank?

SALATHIEL: I can spare twelve thousand pesetas.

JAN: And I'm worth ten times that.

HAILSHAM: I see I'm in the company of giants.

SALATHIEL: But cash id'n all. We need securities, Mr Hailsham.

HAILSHAM *smiles, but says nothing.* JAN *ventures a proposal.*

JAN: I'm prepared to put up Brigan Mine . . .

HAILSHAM *laughs.*

HAILSHAM: Brigan Mine is hardly a goin concern sir. I wouldn't stand Brigan Mine against a three-legged mule.

JAN: It'll be worth a fortune when I get it goin . . .

HAILSHAM: You intend to start it up again do ya?

JAN: Oh yes indeed, there's enough copper under Brigan to plate the whole Atlantic, now the cautious might say keep it underground til the price get yeasty, but I intend to send the army down there and raise ten thousand tons in one big . . .

GONETTA: Dollop.

JAN: . . . flood the market and decimate the competion! After that the price is mine Mr Hailsham. Ours.

HAILSHAM: Good. Well, I'll come in with you on this bank . . .

SALATHIEL: Thass mighty shrewd of ya . . .

HAILSHAM: On these terms. For a fifty-percent interest in Brigan Mine . . .

JAN: Eh?

HAILSHAM: I'll trade with you equal shares in my foundry down at Par, my smelting works in Fowey, my slate quarries in Delabole, my granite excavations in Withiel, my lime pits in Tregadillet, my lead interests in Tavistock, my engineering plant in

Hayle, my Porphry in Roche, my
Academy of Mining in Redruth, my coal
in Porthmeor, my pilchard fleet in
Padstow, my seining company in
Polperro, my boatyard in Wadebridge,
and my viaduct over Looe.

GONETTA: Half built.

HAILSHAM: Soon to be completed.

JAN *leaps from his seat.*

JAN: My Christ Almighty!

HAILSHAM: That should give you all the
securities you need to start a bank.

JAN: An empire! An empire at a stroke!

A rousing ANTHEM *is sung to* JAN:

ANTHEM

Jan May! Emperor!
President of Banks!
Resurrector of Defunct Mines!
Figurehead of Our Times!
Let the Gods be thanked!

REFRAIN

And so it was that this young man,
Who could neither read nor write his
name,
In a matter not of years but hours,
Scaled the highest peaks of power.

ANTHEM

Jan May! Emperor!
Carved in Stone!
Alderman! Burgher! Man of Rank!
Lord of his Domain!
Let the Gods be Thanked!

ACT TWO

TING TANG MINE. *Underground.
Darkness. Candles can be seen moving
about. Men's faces are depicted beneath the
candles. A kibble, a large metal container on
wheels, is pushed towards a pile of rubble.
The men light candles from each others'
candles and set them about the place.*
LISHA, TOM *and* ARTHUR *inspect the
rubble.* RUTTER *is in the distance.*
TREFUSIS *sits some way off, eating his
crib.*
LISHA *picks up stuff from the rubble and
slings it in the kibble.* TOM *inspects the face,*
ARTHUR *sorts through the rubble.*
RUTTER *approaches.*

RUTTER: This your pitch, Thomas May?

TOM: Yes.

RUTTER: What's it lookin like?

ARTHUR: Rich.

RUTTER: Much stuff?

TOM: See for yourself.

RUTTER *moves to the face and inspects it
with* TOM. ARTHUR *picks up a huge
lump of rubble and carries it to the kibble.*

ARTHUR: Look at that Mr Rutter. Solid
ore.

ARTHUR *slings the rock in the kibble
and goes back for another.*

RUTTER: I gotta re-set this pitch.

TOM: Tid'n no richer'n last month.

RUTTER: I know that.

LISHA: Bin runnin like this since Lent.

TREFUSIS (*from a distance*): Before Lent!

RUTTER: I know that.

LISHA: 'Long as you know that.

RUTTER: We can't offer you more'n three
farthin a ton this month.

*At this, everyone stops what they're doing
and looks at* RUTTER. TREFUSIS *stops
eating.*

LISHA: Say that again?

RUTTER: Three farthin.

TOM: Outa the question.

ARTHUR: We'll be diggin two ton a farthin after biddin.

TOM: We can't raise ore at that price. Christ, we're thirty fathoms down.

RUTTER: There's nothin I can do about that.

LISHA: Oo's given ya that thun?

RUTTER: Trice. E came back from the smelters with a big hole in 'is pocket.

TOM: Three farthin a ton? We can't touch the stuff at that price.

RUTTER: Thass up to you mister.

RUTTER *makes off*. LISHA *calls after him:*

LISHA: You can't walk away like that Captain Rutter! If we can't dig it the mine will shut down, then where will you be?

RUTTER *turns and calls back.*

RUTTER: Where will I be? Y'ask where will I be? Huh! I'll be at Brigan! Where will you be?

RUTTER *goes.*

TREFUSIS: You never shoulda sworn that oath. Revelation is a portentous book Thomas. Don't you read your Bible?

LISHA: They gotta whole disbanded regiment under contract diggin ore at Brigan. Dozens and dozens of new shafts bein sunk, place is like a ruddy sieve, we can't compete with that.

TOM: A regiment you say?

LISHA: They march em in from Bodmin every day.

ARTHUR: Bodmin?

LISHA: There's Dolcoath Mine shut down, Binney's, Great Consols is layin men off, they've all gone down Brigan. Tis like a ruddy ant's nest.

TOM: You mean to say there's militia down there, diggin ore? With tributers?

LISHA: All musclin in together, under contract.

MOSES HARVEY *wanders up. A sad man.*

ARTHUR: I avn't eard none a this.

MOSES: I eard it.

TOM: You hear it Moses?

MOSES: Yes.

LISHA: As e re-set your pitch Moses?

MOSES: Yes.

ARTHUR: What price?

MOSES: Penny a ton.

LISHA *throws down his pick.*

MOSES: There's one thing left that we can do.

The others look at him.

MOSES: Pray.

ARTHUR, TOM *and* LISHA *go back to filling the kibble.*

TREFUSIS: On the day you swore that oath your own son fetched ome after nine years in the wilderness bearin great wealth. You shunned that wealth and your son went on to Egypt. Egypt was locked in famine, but Egypt took im to its bosom, and the famine stopped.

TREFUSIS *nods at* TOM *and wanders off.*

MOSES: My pitch is nothing like as rich as this. Lode I'm workin is barren. Tis all quartz. I pick and scrape in search of ore. I offer up a prayer, and lo! There's a fingernail of copper. I ask five shillin a ton for this copper. I seldom get it. Thass one prayer that's never answered . . .
The transaction of cash is a man-made invention, left by the gods for men to sort out amongst themselves. Like a pumpin engine, ave you ever noticed if you pray for a broken engine to work, the gods don't touch it. They'll flood the mine for ya but they'll never pump it out. Thass cus a pumpin engine never grew out the ground, or swam in the sea, or flew in the air. They look down on we and say what the hell are those bastards down there doin with a pumpin engine? We never made one a them in six days! Split the beam with a shaft of lightnin! Bang. The beam's gone. Mine floods. Knacked. All thanks to they selfish bastard gods. And if we defy em? More lightnin. Split again, ead to toe, bloody entrails angin out, food for kites and dogs. Dead if you're lucky. So, there's nothin left to do but pray.

The kibble is full

I've never seen a kibble fill so fast.

ARTHUR: Tid'n worth a bloody farthin.

ARTHUR, TOM *and* LISHA *stand behind the kibble and push it towards the winze. When its momentum is up* TOM *leaves it for the other two to push off and he goes back to pick up tools.*

MOSES: I often pray to a god to make me appy. Burn an animal or summin, sacrifice a rabbit to Appollo or Artemis before I go bed. But I'd still wake up bloody un'appy. I go to work un'appy, I work un'appy, go ome un'appy, trap a rabbit un'appy, burn it un'appy and go bed un'appy.

TOM: You'd be a damn sight appier if you et the rabbit.

MOSES: Tonight when I sacrifice I'll ask the gods to make me angry.

MOSES *wanders off.* TOM *looks round him to check he hasn't left any tools and starts to go.* RUTTER *approaches.*

RUTTER: Mr May.

TOM: What?

RUTTER: When I'm gone to Brigan they're gonna be short of a bal captain ere.

TOM: Whass the point? Bloody bal's dead, whass the point?

RUTTER: They'll need a strong man in front to wind it down.

TOM: Aw, hell.

RUTTER: There's much to be done. There's valuable equipment, machinery, to be raised to grass . . .

TOM: You tellin me this? I was the bugger oo put it down ere.

RUTTER: I'm offerin to recommend ya. Whaddaya say?

RUTTER: Ab'm got no choice ave I, no choice.

RUTTER: Good chap.

RUTTER *goes.* TOM *wanders off.* MOSES *intercepts him.*

MOSES: What did e want?

TOM: E promoted me. To bal captain.

MOSES: See? They invented candles long before they bothered to find out what it was that gave em light.

They go. TREFUSIS *sings:*

TREFUSIS: Have you never bin to Egypt? Tis a short day's walk that way. There's tons of corn in Egypt, And tons more every day.

SENARA *sits by the road leading to* TING TANG. *She is begging.* GONETTA *walks past, she is dressed in her town gear.*

SENARA: Waterloo's won, Boney's crushed, Mr Prussia's on 'is knees, Brittannia rules the . . .

GONETTA: I told you that last month Senara.

SENARA *peers at* GONETTA.

SENARA: Gonetta Bate!

GONETTA: What are you doin ere, sittin in the middle of the road?

SENARA: Beggin.

GONETTA: Ere's a shillin.

SENARA: Where d'e get that?

GONETTA: I'm a banker now, down Trura.

SENARA: You own a bank?

GONETTA: No I run it.

SENARA: Jan May's bank?

GONETTA: I'm the only bugger oo can add up. I got Salathiel Trenannigan sat behind one desk drinkin the profits, Jan May behind another spendin em, and Norman Hailsham givin em away left right and centre to any Whig or Tory oo swear to stamp out the Labour Protection Bill. I run between the three of em pickin up shillins, pourin gin, writin love letters . . .

SENARA: Love letters?

GONETTA: Jan May can't write, neither.

SENARA: Oo's e in love with?

GONETTA: E think e's in love with Ann Roscrow and she with e, but e never get a letter back. Not that I show im anyhow. Dun't wannim jumpin off the cliff.

SENARA: Why not?

GONETTA: I got one ere to deliver.

SENARA: Let's read it?

GONETTA: Costya shillin.

SENARA: Bugger off. You won't find er at Ting Tang anyhow. Ting Tang's shut. Roscrow's off raisin funds to keep the engine pumpin.

GONETTA: That's interesting.

SENARA: She swore an oath on all the books in the Bible that she'd keep the bal pumped dry. I was there when she sweared it. Monday. She was stood up on the Count House steps, Trice behind er, cost-book in 'is 'and, and we was all down there lookin bloody ugly. She said the deal with Sir Richard Crabbe is off. She said the Nanphysic mineral rights ave bin sold, to your lot, for twenty-three pounds. And with that money she was gonna keep Newbolt shaft pumped dry. Take a damn sigh more'n twenty-three pounds, said Moses 'Arvey, e said where's it all gone? E said two months ago this mine was rich! E said where's it all gone? Then Trice opened up the cost book, oh e said, tis all down ere in the cost-book, Mr Harvey, as if that explained it, and Moses leapt! Three foot in the air! And shouted dividends! Tis all leeched out! Bastard dividends! That wun't elp us eat! E roared, we shall ave to break an oath to eat, and where will that land us? Hades, e said, thass where! Hell! Oh said Mrs Roscrow, that depends on the strength of your religious beliefs. Blasphemy! booms out Moses 'Arvey. Trice is quakin now, sweat's raining down on the cost-book, I'll kill for my food, shouts Moses 'Arvey, wavin a bloody ammer up over 'is 'ead, I'll go up on Goss Moor and kill for it! And I think Mrs Roscrow was opin e would, there and then, but e stood where e was and Trice blubbered summin about breakin their oath and goin to Brigan. Moses 'Arvey quivered with rage, all eyes on im, swellin up like this. Bloody ammer gyratin like a windmill, e bellowed, Christ! I'd like to see you swear an oath and bloody break it!

GONETTA: What appenned then?

SENARA: Roscrow swore an oath, She ad to. On all the books in the Bible, including Revelation, that she would do everything she could to keep Ting Tang from floodin, so one day we'd mine copper there again.

GONETTA: Wun't do ya no good, she's agnostic.

SENARA: Well I told y'anyhow.

GONETTA: And I just gave y'a shillin.

SENARA: Thass worth two.

GONETTA: Ere, take the letter.

SENARA: Jan May's love letter?

GONETTA: You'll make a fortune outa that.

GONETTA *gives* SENARA *the love letter and goes off the way she came.* SENARA *calls after her.*

SENARA: Moses 'Arvey dropped dead.

GONETTA: Uh?

SENARA: Right after Mrs Roscrow sweared er oath. E ad apoplectic fit, dropped the ammer on 'is ead, and fell stone dead to the ground.

GONETTA: I arn't payin ya nothing for that, I'm too damned superstitious.

She goes. SENARA *opens the letter and reads it.* TING TANG VILLAGE. SENARA *reads the letter to* YSELLA, *who laughs.* GRAN, BETTY *and* COLAN *are elsewhere, hunched in secret conversation.*

GRAN: There's a consignment of green bananas, from a West Indies ship went down off Pheobe's Point. Close tag's bein kept, and these bananas is headin inland in a sealed wood crate on the back of a mule. A source close to the mule tells me there's a buyer for these bananas in St. Wenn. But progress is slow, by the first mornin these bananas ad'n got no further'n Boscoppa Downs. Next morning they'd reached Carclaze. On my estimation these bananas should be ripe by the time they get to Stenalees, so tis a dash to St. Wenn after that t'avoid em turnin mushy. Possibly transferrin to orse and cart round Coldvreath. This is when they bananas will be at their most vulnerable. I propose an ambush at 'ensbarrer tomorrer night . . . well?

BETTY: I don't ave the stomach for a fight.

GRAN: A mule! Thass all it is! A mule!

BETTY: They'll ave the militia guardin em.

GRAN: Bananas?

COLAN: Militia rides wi' more'n meat now.

BETTY: I saw three militia ridin with a Spaniard oo wad'n carryin nothin more'n a bunch of onions.

GRAN: Gittout!

COLAN: Sure put the kybosh on bananas that do, Gran.

GRAN: They're food! They're fibre! They're fillin!

BETTY: There'll be half Bodmin after they bananas. There'll be limbs torn off and several deaths.

GRAN: Bodmin wouldn' kill for bananas!

BETTY: Thass my vision of hell, walkin round Bodmin inside a somebody's gut.

GRAN: Well!

ARTHUR and TOM *arrive.*

GRAN: Bury im?

TOM: Yes.

GRAN: Poor ole Moses. Young man, never said a foul word to anybody.

TOM: E told me the day before e died that e was goin to ask the gods to make im angry.

GRAN: Well someone shoulda said to im tis us oo make the gods angry.

ARTHUR: Where's Mother?

GRAN: Off.

TOM: Where to?

COLAN: On the scavenge.

GRAN: Gatherin limpets.

ARTHUR: Aw Christ.

COLAN: 'Samatter wi' limpets?

ARTHUR: They're bloody tough and salty.

COLAN: Alright in a pie.

ARTHUR: Gotta fill a pie with a sight more'n limpets to get ridda the salt.

GRAN: She'll pick up a coupla snails on the way back.

GRAN has several sparrows in her lap which she is plucking.

COLAN: Sparrers, Got several sparrers.

GRAN: We id'n puttin these in a pie.

ARTHUR: Why not?

GRAN: I like sparrer baked to a crisp in a hot oven I do. Pop em in your mouth and crunch em up. Only way I'll eat em.

ARTHUR: Put em in a pie! Wun't make no damn difference! There id'n no pastry, stack em on top, they a still burn!

GRAN: I arn't eating sparrers bin on toppa limpets. The salt permeate up.

COLAN: Listen to that. I gotta put up with that all day.

GRAN: You wait till you get to my age.

COLAN: Yes yes yes.

GRAN: I gotta delicate stomach, won't take too much salt.

COLAN: If you didn' ave a gut like an iron foundry you'd be dead by now.

GRAN: Hah! See? Dead! See? It never take long for the conversation to wander round to that!

COLAN: Be one less mouth to feed.

GRAN: Did you hear that?

ARTHUR: E's right. You shoulda died bloody years ago.

They all sit round and ponder what life would be like without GRAN.

COLAN: What about Jan?

TOM: What about im?

COLAN: It's bin my opinion Arthur should make a pilgrimage to Truro and talk to Jan.

ARTHUR: What about?

GRAN: You should do what e did. Go out and tackle the world.

TOM: I'm too old for that.

GRAN: Too old? You're forty-four. You're a captain now, you'd make a damned fortune. They're crying out for mine captains in the Americas.

TOM: Oo told you that?

LISHA wanders up and joins them.

LISHA: Thass true that is.

ARTHUR: If Jan can do it so can we. Think what e was like before e left . . .

GRAN: E was weak.

ARTHUR: And yet e lived through three shipwrecks. And ere we are, sittin ome, waiting for Mother to come back with a basket fulla limpets.

GRAN: Bickerin.

LISHA: Book a passage. Sail across the Atlantic.

GRAN: Send the money back.

LISHA: I know where to go. Michigan. They got a copper belt there wide as Europe.

ARTHUR: What about it?

TOM: Well, if Jan can do it . . .

GRAN: Exactly!

ARTHUR: Yes!

They all stand. MAUDE *enters with a bag.* ARTHUR *goes off and comes on with more bags while* MAUDE *and* BETTY *fuss round* TOM *and* LISHA, *preparing them for their journey.* YESELLA *and* SENARA, *the letter finished, walk off across the stage, picking out the good bits of the letter and laughing:*

SENARA: 'The only time we ever met I was soppin wet . . .'

YSELLA: 'O cursed winds that keep us apart . . .'

SENARA: 'Let us collide in matrimony . . .'

YSELLA: 'I'd crawl to Moscow, To meet Mrs Roscrow . . .'

FALMOUTH HARBOUR. ARTHUR, TOM *and* LISHA *wander through the crowds,* MAUDE *and* BETTY *in attendance.* TREFUSIS *sings while* MAUDE *bids her farewells.*

TREFUSIS: Have you never bin to Michigan?
It's a short walk up a plank,
Nothin more, nothin less,
We're goin to meet the Yank!

Have you never crossed an ocean?
Tis a sit out on the deck,
Nothin more, nothin less,
We won't break our neck!

Have you never travelled far from home?

It's an amble in the breeze.
Nothin more, nothin less,
A skate across the seas.

And when we get to Michigan?
We're goin to break the bank,
Nothin more, nothin less,
Cus we're goin to meet the Yank!

The sound and bustle of a busy embarcation can be seen and heard. BETTY *is very emotional, mopping up her tears with a handkerchief, consoled by* LISHA.

ARTHUR: Goodbye Mother.

MAUDE: Goodbye boy.

MAUDE *hugs* ARTHUR.

ARTHUR: C'mon Mother.

MAUDE *leaves* ARTHUR *and hugs* TOM.

MAUDE: Goodbye Tom.

TOM: Goodbye Maude.

MAUDE *clings to* TOM.

ARTHUR: C'mon Father.

TOM: C'mon Maude.

MAUDE: Goodbye dear.

TOM *gently parts from* MAUDE *and* ARTHUR *prizes* BETTY *from* LISHA. TOM, ARTHUR *and* LISHA *wave to* MAUDE *and* BETTY *as they walk up the gangplank and depart.* MAUDE *and* BETTY *are left alone.* BETTY *sobs:*

BETTY: Tis your damn son oo's done this. Jan May. Im and 'is bank, and 'is Brigan. I knew when e come ome e was up to mischief.

MAUDE: Come on Betty, stop bein so damn miserable . . .

BETTY: Look, there's men ere from all over the district, bein shoved off to sea by your son Jan . . .

Exit MAUDE *and* BETTY. *An* ANTHEM *is sung.*

ANTHEM: The Worshipful Jan May Esquire!
Lord High Sherrif of the Shire!
Honoured Guest at Public Functions!
Top of the Table at Civic Luncheons!
Chief Executive of Justice!
Loved by all but sadly, loveless!

JAN, GONETTA *and* SALATHIEL *sit in the boardroom of* JAN's *bank. The room is vast, with* SALATHIEL *sitting at her desk one end, counting money, stamping a ledger and drinking gin, and* JAN *the other, his feet up on his desk, picking his tie.* GONETTA *polishes brass.*

SALATHIEL: Gonetta. More gin.

GONETTA *fills* SALATHIEL's *glass.*

JAN: So there's nothin like a pumpin engine.

SALATHIEL: Yes.

JAN: Tis a speculator's dream.

SALATHIEL: Exactly.

JAN: Cus the value of a mine, no matter how much copper's stored below grass, is nothing more nor less than the market price of its pumpin engine.

SALATHIEL: That's the theory.

JAN: Cus if the pumpin engine stop pumpin, the mine floods and becomes worthless!

SALATHIEL: Bravo. More gin Gonetta. Run rabbit!

GONETTA *pours gin.*

JAN: So if some Mineowner travelled to Truro, and wandered in here at the bank one day and said to we, Mr May, Mr Trenannigan, Mr . . . where is e?

GONETTA: Hailsham? E's up in London, residin at the Saracen's Head, Petitionin Castlereagh and Liverpool about their buggerin Labour Protection Bill. Lashin em with 'is dogfish tongue.

JAN: That should do some good.

SALATHIEL: . . . 'the price of copper's 'it rock bottom. I can't produce no longer. My mine is up for sale. Any takers . . .'

JAN: We say . . .

SALATHIEL: What's the price of your pumpin engine!

JAN: You got it.

SALATHIEL: 'Oh but Mr May, my mine's worth more'n that, why there's a thousand tons a copper just ten fathoms below adit level . . .'

JAN: But without your pumpin engine . . .

SALATHIEL: To preserve it from floodin . . .

JAN: Tis worthless!

GONETTA: It's bloody cruel . . .

SALATHIEL: More gin.

JAN: Gonetta.

GONETTA: Yup?

JAN: Read me my engagements for tonight.

GONETTA: Tonight you're the Guest of Honour at the Loyal Friends of Freedom's Anniversary Celebration of the Fall of the Systematic Engines of Corruption and Disorder at the Public Rooms. Before that you're judgin pies for the Only The Sober Circle of Women's fund-raisin at the Jesuit Seminary.

JAN: Tell me the time.

GONETTA *takes* SALATHIEL's *watch from her waistcoat and squints at it.*

GONETTA: Five o'clock.

JAN *stretches.*

JAN: Fill me a bath.

GONETTA *unhooks a bath from the wall, lays it on the floor and unfolds an exotic Chinese screen around it. She sets about filling the bath behind the screen.*

JAN: It's my opinion agitators should be shot. Thass my opinion. And I've let it be known to the bench. If we ad'n brung in the militia down at Withiel there woulda bin mayhem. Lumpsa granite flying through windows, quarriers rampagin through the streets, but no. We called in the militia, one man was killed, and peace reigned. I ope Mr Hailsham does some good with this Castlereagh. Damned Protection Bill. Tis we oo need protectin.

GONETTA: Bath's ready.

JAN *goes behind the screen.* SALATHIEL *drains her gin and follows him, rolling up her sleeves as she goes. Clothes appear draped over the screen as* JAN *is undressed.* GONETTA *finds herself a cigar and lights it. There is a knock at the door, and unknown to the others,* GONETTA *goes to answer it during* JAN's *speech.*

JAN: I shall make it the centrepiece of my speech tonight before the Friends of

Freedom. The Labour Protection Bill. Where will it end? Its effect on the creation and distribution of wealth. The role of the militia. The defence of the pocket. Yes. My lord, ladies and gentlemen, Loyal Friends of Freedom. 'The defence of the pocket. My power is in my pocket. My trousers bulge with it. I can take it out, whenever I like, and disseminate it across the county. On the other 'and I can keep it where it is and watch it grow. This is Freedom, Loyal Friends, we'll not be blackmailed by those who see it as their right to dip their own grubby hands into my pocket. And take out whatever they like, whenever they like!'

ROSCROW *has been admitted by* GONETTA *and she stands listening to this. She speaks quietly to* GONETTA.

ROSCROW: Have I come at a difficult time?

GONETTA: No.

JAN (*behind screen*): What?

GONETTA: I said no!

JAN (*behind screen*): How d'ya mean, no?!

GONETTA: No she ab'm come at a difficult time!

JAN (*behind screen*): Who?!

GONETTA: Ann Roscrow!

JAN: WHAT!

A giant splash behind the screen and JAN's *naked, wet torso appears over the top.*

JAN: Aw my God! Jesus Christ in hellfire!

He disappears and his clothes are wrenched from the top of the screen.

ROSCROW: I think I should go.

GONETTA: Stay and ave some gin.

ROSCROW: Thank you no.

GONETTA: Siddown.

JAN (*behind screen*): Get riddofer!

ROSCROW: I'll go. I'll come back. I should have made an appointment.

GONETTA: E's that busy you're lucky to of catched im in the bath without Hailsham.

ROSCROW: Well there's that. Yes. Perhaps I'll stay.

ROSCROW *sits.* GONETTA *pours two glasses of gin.* GONETTA *drinks hers and offers the other to* ROSCROW, *who refuses it.*

ROSCROW: I don't drink.

GONETTA: Pity.

GONETTA *drinks* ROSCROW's *gin.* JAN *appears fully clothed from behind the screen. His shirt and trousers are wet. He walks with his arms and legs akimbo, much as he did when he first met* ROSCROW. ROSCROW *rises.* SALATHIEL *emerges from behind the screen and crosses to her desk. She sits and continues counting money.*

JAN: Mrs Roscrow . . .

He crosses to greet her.

ROSCROW: Good evening Mr May.

JAN: Huh! Why is it every time we meet I'm soakin wet?

ROSCROW: I won't stay long.

JAN (*to* GONETTA): Gimme a gin. Give er a gin.

ROSCROW: Thank you I don't drink.

JAN *sits uncomfortably in his seat.* GONETTA *furnishes him with a gin and replenishes* SALATHIEL's *glass. She finds a chair for* ROSCROW.

GONETTA: Y'allowed to siddown?

ROSCROW: Thank you.

She sits.

JAN: State your business, Mrs Roscrow.

ROSCROW: I've come to ask you for a loan.

JAN: A loan?

ROSCROW: Ting Tang is in desperate trouble.

JAN: I didn't know that.

ROSCROW: I'm sure you didn't.

SALATHIEL: We id'n a lendin bank Madam. We'm a depositary.

ROSCROW (*confidentially, to* JAN): You don't understand Mr May. I ask it as a special request. A personal favour. From your own pocket.

JAN: I'm very flattered Mrs Roscrow. Very taken. Tis only the second time I've met you and here you are, askin me personal favours.

SALATHIEL: If e went round dishin out cash to every tinpot bal owner e'd met twice e'd be bankrupt, Madam.

JAN: Oh yes this is a special, a personal request.

SALATHIEL: They all say that . . .

JAN: You don't understand . . .

ROSCROW: I considered that under the circumstances . . .

JAN: See there's circumstances . . .

SALATHIEL: Come ere.

JAN *rises and waddles over to* SALATHIEL.

SALATHIEL *(confidential, to* JAN): The only way you can elp er is to offer to buy the place, and then for nothin more than the worth of its pumpin engine. £25. We've bin through all this. That is all that bal's worth. Its pumpin engine.

JAN: There's circumstances.

SALATHIEL: What circumstances?

JAN: We love each other.

SALATHIEL: Who?

JAN: Me and er.

SALATHIEL *(surprised)*: She loves you?

JAN: We fell in love the first time ever we set eyes on each other.

SALATHIEL: And she got the bald audacity to come in ere and beg you to bail er out cus you love each other? That id'n circumstances Mr May. Thass blackmail.

JAN: Blackmail?

SALATHIEL: Call er bluff.

JAN: How?

SALATHIEL: Offer to marry er.

JAN: You think I should? Oh yes!

SALATHIEL: Marry er and you get Ting Tang by default, without partin with a penny piece.

JAN: Oh Zeus! Two dead birds wi' one stone!

SALATHIEL: After all you're a man of passion, you've met er twice, tis 'igh time you got wed.

JAN *takes up his glass and returns to* ROSCROW. *On his way he passes* GONETTA *who hands him her cigar. He takes it and sits opposite* ROSCROW. *Puffs on his cigar.*

JAN: Mrs Roscrow.

ROSCROW: Yes?

JAN: Anne.

ROSCROW: Yes?

JAN: Will you marry me?

ROSCROW: I beg your pardon?

JAN: Marry me, Anne.

ROSCROW *(staggered)*: I think I need a glass of gin.

GONETTA *rustles up a glass of gin.* JAN *follows* GONETTA *as she scuttles about the place.*

JAN: Whass the matter with the woman?

GONETTA: I can't imagine.

JAN: We fell in love. Good God a day asn't passed when I havn't dreamed of marriage to the woman half a dozen times.

GONETTA: The vanity of the man.

JAN: Vanity? Vanity?

ROSCROW *drains her gin and stands.*

ROSCROW: Did it never cross your mind the circumstances I spoke of might have been the hardship of your mother, and your sisters, your grandmother and blind brother?

SALATHIEL: Bugger them . . .

JAN: They wouldn't take my money. They wouldn't take it, d'you hear? They turned their stupid ignorant backs upon it. That's the truth!

ROSCROW: They didn't know what to do with it, just like you, Mr May. Your father had a linny to build. Thirty seven shillings saved, that was his fortune, that was his great achievement.

SALATHIEL: Look, e's a busy man . . .

JAN: Yes, a busy man.

GONETTA: E loaf about all day . . .

SALATHIEL: Stuck ere in Trura . . .

JAN: Here in the bank . . .

SALATHIEL: Guest of honour ere and there tis a different damn world.

JAN: How d'ya expect me to follow their every damn move?

SALATHIEL: They didn't want 'is money, you 'eard im.

JAN: They couldn't care less if I'd gone to the world or, or . . .

SALATHIEL: Gone to Jesus.

JAN: I'm different to them, I'm a man of the world . . .

SALATHIEL: They're ignorant, little people.

JAN: Yes!

SALATHIEL: E's a successful, proud man. E offered it to em once and they scorned im. Like the ingrate, broad-horizons narrow-minded hard-hearted granite-headed bastards they've always bin down Ting Tang. He's a Brigan man now, pure and simple, and Brigan people dun't talk to Ting Tang people, Brigan people dun't meddle with their affairs, cus Brigan people's better'n Ting Tang people, cus Ting Tang people's the meanest, leastest people who ever crawled on their bellies across God's earth!

SALATHIEL, *the worst for gin, promptly falls asleep.*
GONETTA *crosses to her and inspects her.*

GONETTA: She's gin-distant.

ROSCROW *is recovering from the assault.*

GONETTA: You alright?

ROSCROW *nods.*

GONETTA: 'Nother gin?

ROSCROW: I swore an oath.

GONETTA: You just broke it so ave another.

ROSCROW: I swore on every book in the Bible that I would do everything I could to keep Ting Tang open. If I refuse your offer of marriage Mr May I break the oath. Well that doesn't trouble me. I don't believe for one minute that I shall rot in hell, but there are people in Ting Tang who do. They've taken great risks because of it. One person has died as a result. And those who are left will suffer far more than I will ever suffer if I marry another man I don't love. Another ridiculous man.

JAN (*to* GONETTA): What does she mean? She gonna marry me? What does she mean?

GONETTA: You don't ave to marry im.

JAN: Oh yes she does, now you shuttup Gonetta, you done enough damage. Leave er be . . .

GONETTA: Just tell im about 'is father and brother . . .

JAN: Eh?

GONETTA: Go on, tell im where they've gone.

JAN: What? Where?

ROSCROW: They've gone to the world.

JAN: Oh no.

GONETTA: But you don't want to hear about them, the meanest, leastest people who ever crawled on their bellies across God's earth . . .

JAN: Tell me, where've they gone?

GONETTA: Plenty a time for them when you're married and dishin out your frozen charity . . .

JAN: Tell me!

The sound of a hymn can be heard. The atmosphere changes. A PREACHER *can be seen standing under a tree, a gin bottle hidden behind him.* MAUDE, GRAN, BETTY ELDER *and* COLAN *kneel before the preacher.* HE *speaks as the hymn is sung.*

HYMN: Sing from the chamber to the grave,
I hear the dying miner say,
A sound of melody I crave,
Upon my burial day.

Sing sweetly as you travel on,
And keep the funeral slow,
The angels sing where I am gone,
And you shall sing below.

Then bear me gently to the grave,

And as you pass along,
Remember twas my wish to have,
A pleasant funeral song.

The PREACHER'*s sermon can be heard
during the hymn.*

PREACHER: Great Og and Agog, where
are e?
Where now is Lot! At Zoar safe?
And his wife? A pillar! Salt for pilchers!
Come down! Come down thou great
Jehovah! Scat these hard hearts!
Scat the granite hearts of these hellborn
savages!

JAN: Where are we?

GONETTA: Goss Moor.

JAN: Who's dead? Who's died?
Tell me!

GONETTA: This is a service of
remembrance.

JAN: Who for?

GONETTA: Your father. Tom. He met his
death in Michigan. Or so they say. It
might of course not be true.

The service is over. MAUDE *and*
BETTY *start their journey home.* BETTY
is in floods of tears and MAUDE *comforts
her.*

MAUDE: Come on Betty. Tom id'n dead!
E ad'n died! Jan didn' die, did e! They all
said Jan was dead an I said e wad'n. Tom
id'n dead!E a turn up one day, out the
blue, just like Jan.

JAN: Aw Christ e's dead Mother! E's dead!
Don't you understand, you stupid
woman, e's dead! Listen to me!

GONETTA: She can't ear ya! You id'n ere!

MAUDE *stands alone, on a headland,
looking out to sea.*

JAN: Where are we now?

GONETTA: Rame Head. She comes out
here every day, waiting for Tom's boat to
return.

JAN: Why dun't somebody tell er Thomas
is dead! Why can't somebody tell er I
never left these shores? I lied to er!
Somebody tell er that! Somebody tell her
to wake up! Somebody tell er to face the
truth for a change! Christ if somebody
told er that none a this would've
appenned!

GONETTA: Of course you was
shipwrecked.

JAN: No!

GONETTA: You told er that. You told er
you survived three shipwrecks.

JAN: One. I witnessed one. I never left
these shores!

JAN *tells his story to* MAUDE, *who
doesn't hear him.* GONETTA *and*
ROSCROW *look on.*

JAN: I'd bin up Plymouth, the big do they
ad up there when Bonaparte was
anchored in the Sound? I was rough as
rats. I adn' et for three days. I was sleepin
in hedges. I resolved to walk home, back
along the coast to see what I could pick up
off the beaches . . . I got some way down
and fetched up at Ropehaven one night.
You know Ropehaven?

GONETTA: No.

ROSCROW: I do.

JAN: I walked straight through the place
and bedded down behind a hedge at a
remote, uninhabited place called Fox
Cove. On the edge of a cliff. When I woke
it was thick fog. Early morning. There
was a breeze, blowin onshore, and the fog
hung over the water round the cliff. Did I
say I was alone?

GONETTA: No?

JAN: Well, I wasn't. I thought I was, but I
wasn't.

*A voice can be heard through the fog. It is
the voice of* BLAKE, *a member of a ship's
crew. He speaks quietly, without fuss.*

BLAKE: She's paying off sir.

CAPTAIN: Let her wind round on her
heels.

BLAKE: Hard over.

JAN *is now apart from* GONETTA *and*
ROSCROW, *next to* MAUDE, *on his
belly, looking over the cliff.*

JAN: There was no panic in their voices.
Commands were spoken. Voices carry far
across water.

CAPTAIN: Let go the peak halyard.

JAN: I could see nothin.

CAPTAIN: Take a sounding by the bow.

HOYLE: Four fathom, sir. We're finding rock.

CAPTAIN: Sound aft.

BLAKE: She's veering.

CAPTAIN: Bring the wind aft.

BLAKE: Hard to starb'd.

MARTYN: Three fathoms aft!

HOYLE: Rocks on the larb'd quarter!

SOAMES: Rocks to starb'd!

CAPTAIN: Let go anchors! Both bowyers! Keep her apeak! Tackle up the sheet and let go aft! Reef the t'gallants!

JAN: The anchors splashed, and the sails slatted the masts. All this I was able to hear quite clearly. The breeze had freshened and the fog begun to lift. Suddenly I was able to see a brig schooner, lyin uneasily about a mile offshore, smack between two rocks.

CAPTAIN: Weigh anchors! Set the stays'ls! Set the t'gallants! We'll wear her out Mr Blake!

BLAKE: Brace the yards!

JAN: Close hauled, she managed to sail more or less straight out to sea. I nearly lost sight of er, but by now the wind was blowin a near gale, and in less time she took to wear the two miles out to sea, the wind blew her back again!

BLAKE: Furl the t'gallants! Haul it to the yard!

HOYLE: Buntline's parted!

SOAMES: Foretack's parted!

CAPTAIN: Heave her to!

BLAKE: Clew up the main tops'l! She's slattin! Put down the wheel! Head her! Head her!

MARTYN: Stays'l's parted!

By now the sound of wind and sea are very loud. The voices are desperate shouts.

CAPTAIN: We must cut away the foremast! Its the only way to head her! Mr Blake! Cut the weather shrouds!

BLAKE: Down from the rigging! Topmen! Down from the rigging there!

HOYLE: The rudder's dismounted! She's took the sternframe to bits!

CAPTAIN: Jury rig it best you can!

BLAKE: Come down topmen!

CAPTAIN: Martyn! Hoyle! Soames! Help Mr Blake there! Look out!

BLAKE: Let got the port boryer!

JAN: Her anchor dragged! They couldn't save her!

HOYLE: Make sternway!

CAPTAIN: Let go the starb'd boryer!

HOYLE: That's no bastard good!

SOAMES: We're stoked in the bilges!

BLAKE: She's splittin open!

JAN: She was back on the rocks!

CAPTAIN: Sling over the boats!

JAN: The ship broke up!

The storm dies down.

JAN: It was nearly dark but I could see the bodies and debris washin in. Cargo, luggage, utensils, tangled rope, everything you could name. Poultry, dogs. The boats capsized, men were flung this way and that, broken bodies were washed up, and I made my way down the cliff to the beach.

JAN walks on the beach. He is surrounded by what he described, bodies and debris.

JAN: I was still alone. Huge breakers crashed and pulled. Bodies bent backwards over double were tossed and shaken like straw.

JAN walks among the bodies. He checks to see if they're dead. He finds a carpet bag, and a trunk full of clothes, uniforms, neckerchiefs, and boots. He hears a sound. He is terrified. He finds the body from which it emanates. JAN looks up at GONETTA, *who sits on* SALATHIEL's *desk.*

JAN: God in heaven forgive me for what I did next. Jesus don't turn your back on me.

The MAN *who made the sound crawls towards a box which is sealed and watertight. He falls across the box. JAN rolls him off the box, and, finding a stone, breaks it open. The box is full of money.*

The MAN *weakly attempts to clutch at the box.* JAN *raises the stone and brings it down on the* MAN's *head, killing him.* JAN *throws the rock into the sea and shovels the contents of the box into the carpet bag. He squeezes clothes into the carpet bag and changes into those which won't fit into the bag. He climbs wearily up the cliff.* MAUDE *is still there, looking out across the sea.*

JAN: I cut away from the coast and journeyed across Goss Moor. The first person I met, the first living person I met, was my Mother.

JAN *and* MAUDE *stand opposite each other, as far away from each other as possible.* MAUDE *sits on the bank of the river, removing her boots.* ROSCROW *has left the bank,* SALATHIEL *is still slumped across her desk,* GONETTA *sits on the edge of the desk, swinging her legs.* HAILSHAM *bursts through the door of the bank, his cloak swirling.*

HAILSHAM: Gonetta!

GONETTA: Welcome back.

HAILSHAM: Disaster!

GONETTA: Bad news?

HAILSHAM (*indicates* SALATHIEL): Wake im up! Where's Jan May? Labour Protection Bill's bin voted through! We got riots in the lime pits! Tavistock's under siege, they've gone on strike in Brigan, the pilchard fleet's sunk, the viaduct's collapsed over Looe!

GONETTA: Is that all?

HAILSHAM: There's worse! The potato crop's failed. there's a thousand farmers marchin this way, demandin their cash back! Where's Jan May, we gotta quell em! Where's e to?

GONETTA: I could say e's judgin pies . . .

HAILSHAM: Judgin pies? At a time like this?

GONETTA: But e id'n.

HAILSHAM: Thank God for that!

GONETTA: I could say e's guest of honour at the Friends of Freedom.

HAILSHAM: That won't help us now . . .

GONETTA: But e id'n . . .

HAILSHAM: Thass enough conundrum Gonetta, where's e got to!

GONETTA *points* JAN *out to* HAILSHAM.

HAILSHAM: Oh no, no, no!

He watches JAN *call across the river to* MAUDE.

JAN: Mother? That you Mother?

MAUDE *looks up and sees* JAN *on the opposite bank.*

MAUDE: Jan?

MAUDE *starts to wade across the river to* JAN.

JAN: I'm comin ome Mother, for good.

HAILSHAM *starts.*

HAILSHAM: What?!

HAILSHAM *shakes* SALATHIEL.

MAUDE: For good? Why dear? Whatever for?

HAILSHAM: Mr Trenannigan! Wake up!

JAN: I've heard all about it, Mother.

HAILSHAM: Wake up blast ya! We're ruined!

JAN: Ting Tang, Arthur, and Tom.

GONETTA: She's bin like that for three days.

JAN: I'm comin ome to make sure it never appen again.

MAUDE: But Jan, it id'n likely to.

HAILSHAM: Wake up! The farmers are comin!

SALATHIEL *wakes.* MAUDE *has reached the* BRIGAN *side of the river,* SALATHIEL *slowly comes to.*

HAILSHAM: Our empire's in tatters, Jan May's deserted us, we gotta get im back, it's our only hope . . .

SALATHIEL *rises and heads for the door.*

HAILSHAM: Back door! There's farmers stormin the front!

SALATHIEL, HAILSHAM *and* GONETTA *exit through the back of the bank.*

MAUDE: Jan, we got news your father

died. In Michigan.

JAN: I heard that.

MAUDE: Oh you heard that. Well there's no truth in it. I said e id'n dead! I said e's too good! I said God give im life and e'll die natural when is age come up. I said e's too damned good to die young. I suppose you want ferryin?

JAN: No, Mother. Bless you no. Clamber on my back, I'll see you across.

MAUDE *hops on* JAN's *back and he starts to wade across.* HAILSHAM, SALATHIEL *and* GONETTA *arrive, breathless, at the* BRIGAN *bank of the river.*

HAILSHAM: Hoy! Jan May!

MAUDE: Jan, your brother Arthur and Lisha Ball sent a package back from Michigan. You know what was in it?

JAN *speeds up his crossing, away from* HAILSHAM, *who arrives, breathless at the* BRIGAN *bank.*

HAILSHAM: Jan! Come ere! Come back! You can't abandon us now! You're a ruined man if you cross this river!

JAN *stops, midstream.*

JAN: What was in the package Mother?

MAUDE: Gold.

HAILSHAM: Gold!

SALATHIEL: Gold!

HAILSHAM *scrambles into the river, stumbling and crawling across on his knees.* SALATHIEL *hops onto* GONETTA's *back and urges her across like a horse.*

JAN: Gold!

JAN *drops* MAUDE *in the river.* BETTY ELDER *arrives.*

BETTY: Jan, you ear 'bout the gold? Damned great nugget big as your fist!

MAUDE: You stupid wilful boy! Get me up! Look at this! Soaked!

GRAN *arrives with* COLAN. COLAN *pulls a cart and* GRAN *leads him.* GRAN *carries a big stick.* GRAN *lowers the side of the cart to reveal a huge nugget of gold sitting in the cart.* HAILSHAM *stops dead on his knees in the river and* GONETTA,

with SALATHIEL *on her back, falls oer him. Everybody stares at the gold.*

GRAN: Jan, I gotta great lumpa gold ere, I want ya to weight it for me and get it assayed.

MAUDE: Get me up. Get me up! I can't get up!

HAILSHAM *clambers to his feet.*

HAILSHAM: Jan, we'll do good business with this gold. Now dun't be hasty, tis all we need to get us back on our feet again Jan, don't throw it away . . .

GRAN *strides into the river with her stick.*

MAUDE: Please! Somebody! Help me!

ROSCROW *arrives on the* TING TANG *bank of the river and wakes in to assist* MAUDE. GRAN, *a formidable adversary, holds her stick across* HAILSHAM's *chest, barring his way.*

GRAN: You want gold? You go to Michigan and dig it.

HAILSHAM: Call er off!

GRAN *pushes* HAILSHAM *back towards the* BRIGAN *bank of the river. She threatens him with her stick.* HAILSHAM *considers his chances, then turns to* GONETTA:

HAILSHAM: Gonetta.

GONETTA: What?

HAILSHAM: Book me a ticket. To Michigan.

HAILSHAM *turns on his heels and runs.* GRAN *stands over* SALATHIEL.

GRAN: I know you! You're Grace Briney!

SALATHIEL *studies* GRAN.

SALATHIEL: Aw my God!

SALATHIEL *scrambles to her feet.*

GRAN: Three decades I bin untin you! You and Dasher! Where's that money I gived ya! Where's it to?

SALATHIEL *starts to run off towards where* HAILSHAM *has gone.* ROSCROW *has wrapped* MAUDE *in her cloak and is going off with her.* JAN *yells:*

JAN: Mrs Roscrow! Wait!

This stops everybody in their tracks.

SALATHIEL, HAILSHAM,
ROSCROW, MAUDE, BETTY,
COLAN, GRAN. JAN *is the only one left
in the river.*

JAN: Mrs Roscrow. Anne. I stand before
you a humble, contrite man with nothin
more in the world than the suit I stand up
in. I gotta big heart though, and
underneath it all I arn't bad to look at.
Won't you marry me now?

All eyes turn to ROSCROW.

ROSCROW: It's well-known that my last
marriage was unhappy and ill-matched,
Mr May.

JAN: Oh I accept you're difficult to live with
Mrs Roscrow . . .

ROSCROW: After my husband died I
emerged from a brief period of mourning
to hear the story going round that I'd
killed him.

JAN: I can defend myself!

ROSCROW: You know how rumour, that
rife weed, is soon taken to the garden and
grown as truth. I was expelled from the
Only The Sober Circle of Women, and
branded a witch by the Tent Methodists.
The Bible Christians reckoned me a man
dressed as a woman, and quoted as proof
the lack of children . . .

JAN: Show me 'ow to do it and I'll prove em
wrong!

ROSCROW: I did nothing to deny it
because I was too busy reviving my
fortunes. My husband only left me his
share in Ting Tang, his money perished
with him.

JAN: Perished?

ROSCROW: His skull had been shattered
by a rock. The storm was so violent and
the shipwreck so complete that we
assumed the cause of death to have been
the force of nature. Perhaps it was. He
was a brutal man, his death was quite
fitting, and the freedom it brought me has
filled me with a profound love of life, Mr
May. And I have no-one to thank more
than you.

JAN (*whispers to* GONETTA): What does
she mean? She gonna marry me? Well is
she?

GONETTA: She won't if she's got any
sense.

MAUDE: I wish you would marry im, bring
im down to earth.

COLAN: You owe im a favour.

SALATHIEL: I spent the night with im, e
wun't let ya down.

GRAN: Marry the bugger and let's get ome.

BETTY: E ab'm got no brain, you could
convert im to whatever you like.

ROSCROW: I have to admit . . .

JAN: What?

ROSCROW: You are different to what I
thought you were when I first met you.

JAN (*to* GONETTA): Is that good?

GONETTA: It's gettin better.

ROSCROW: And in time you might
become quite acceptable. Yes.

JAN: Oh, joy!

GONETTA: In time.

ROSCROW: I propose a period of
betrothal, with an annulment clause on
both sides.

JAN (*to* GONETTA): How's that?

GONETTA: It's as good as you're gonna
get. (*To* ROSCROW.) We accept.

*A sigh of relief from all
An* ANTHEM *is sung to* JAN:

ANTHEM: Jan May! Lovesick Man!
Fortune's come and fortune's gone!
Welcome home again!

*JAN hops on GONETTA's back and she
carries him towards* TING TANG.

THE DEAD MONKEY

The Dead Monkey was first performed by the Royal Shakespeare Company at The Pit, London on 1 July 1986. The cast was as follows:

VET	Antony O'Donnel
DOLORES	Frances Barber
HANK	Bruce Alexander
Directed by	Roger Michell
Music composed by	Jeremy Sams
Designed by	Chris Townsend

Production Note

The monkey belongs to a numerous species, the choice of size and colour is wide. When casting a specimen to star in this play it is essential that the monkey in question should be big enough to have done to Dolores what she said it did, and to have died as a result of it. There is a species in Japan which fits the bill: it is very large and has a bright pink lecherous face with a permanent expression of horror.

ACT ONE

Scene One

*The kitchen/diner of a small wood shack
close by a beach in California.
The furniture is cheap. There is a table, two
chairs, and an easy chair. A large Frigidaire.
Against a wall there is a pile of magazines:
'Harpers and Queen'.
There are copies of the magazine scattered on
the floor, in strategic places.
There is a bowl of oranges and an orange
crusher.
The kitchenette is partitioned off from the
main room.
There is a window in the partition, and a
bead curtain in the door.
The bedroom, off, is beyond the kitchenette.*

*A dead monkey lies on the table.
It is half covered with an Indian blanket.
A woman, DOLORES, paces the floor.
She is agitated.
A VET inspects the monkey with his
stethoscope.
He covers the monkey with the blanket and
folds his stethoscope.*

DOLORES: Is he dead?

VET: Oh yes. He's dead.

DOLORES: Oh God. Oh God.

VET: He died of natural causes Mrs
Wandaback. He was an old monkey.

DOLORES: What shall I do?

VET: With the monkey? You have several
options. You could bury him, we have an
animal cemetery in a pleasant corner of
the zoo. Costya forty dollars. Or you
could have him cremated, costya little
more.

DOLORES: What the hell's Hank gonna
say? It'll break his heart.

VET: Or you could eat him. Monkey flesh is
considered a delicacy.

DOLORES: . . . break his heart.

VET: There's a lotta people consider it an
honour for the monkey. To be eaten by
ah. By Mummy and Daddy.

DOLORES: I couldn't eat it.

VET: It's a trying time for you Mrs
Wandaback. If you just pay me my fee,

$24.60 I'll sneak out and leave you to your
bereavement . . .

DOLORES: Yes. The fee.

*She hunts in a shoulder bag which hangs
over the back of a chair. She finds a couple
of dollars. She then proceeds to find
money all over the room, inside an empty
cookie jar, amongst the oranges, amongst
the magazines, in the fridge. Finally she
amasses $24.*

You've cleaned me out. Could I mail you
the sixty cents? I'm expecting my husband
home, he brings home the bacon in this
family . . .

VET: That's fine . . .

DOLORES: Such as it is.

VET: We'll forget the sixty cents Mrs
Wandaback.

DOLORES: You're very kind. Could you
reserve a place in the cemetery for the
monkey? I'm sure Hank will wanna see
him given a decent burial.

VET: Popular choice Mrs Wandaback. It's
a lovely, quiet little spot, right by the
armadillo house. And for another $35 we
provide a headstone of your choice.
According to religion.

DOLORES: Oh, that's nice. Hank will
appreciate that.

VET: What religion does your husband
follow?

DOLORES: He's an atheist but I know he
will adopt something for this.

VET: Have him come in and see the range
before he makes a choice. I'd advise
against Buddhism. Buddhas cost and they
tend to get stolen.

DOLORES: Thank you. You've been a
great help.

VET: I try to be.

He starts to go.

Oh . . .

DOLORES: Yes?

VET: Should you decide on another
monkey, we have plenty in stock, right by
the dolphinarium.

DOLORES: Thank you. I'll inform Hank
of that.

The VET *goes.*
DOLORES *fixes herself a drink, a dash of vodka with the product of a crushed orange. She goes and uncovers the monkey down to the neck.*

Poor little monkey. I did all I could. Old age. Well, that'll do for Hank. I sure dunno what he's gonna say. When he left y'a week ago, you was jumpin up and down, chattering away, playing ball with him in the garden, scratching your underarms, a healthy monkey. He'll just never believe you're dead. You were always Hank's little monkey. I could never figure out why, as soon as Hank left the house, you so completely altered your personality. I had no idea it was within a monkey's physiogomy to do that. But I guess it was because he was your brother. I grew to love you in the end. Sad as hell you're dead. Sad as hell. Christ I'm, so sad. Goodbye little monkey. I love ya . . .

She covers him.
A door slams out back.
HANK *enters.*
He is a big, rangy guy. He is awkwardly dressed in a salesman's suit. He is tired and grimy. He walks straight to the easy chair and flops.

HANK: Hullo sweet.

DOLORES: Hullo Hank.

HANK *rises. He kisses* DOLORES *full on the mouth. he is horny. When he has finished with her,* DOLORES *asks:*

How was your trip?

HANK: My trip? It was a journey through a whore's soiled undergarments.

DOLORES: Gee I'm sorry to hear that Hank.

HANK: No it was good.

DOLORES: You made a lotta sales?

HANK: I sold all my stock. And more. But who the fuck to? Sharks. Leeches. Assholes. And what for Dolores? To pay off my company debts! Christ there are guys out there look at me and say he's so dumb that Hank he thinks a Mexican border pays rent.

DOLORES: Oh Hank honey, they don't.

HANK: Plain as a lead pipe.

He vigorously squeezes oranges into the juicer.

You know what I think of the world Dolores? This thought revolves around my head when I'm gunning down the freeway. The centre of the world is a monkey's asshole. Every time the monkey shits the world contracts a little bit. Shits some more and the skin draws tighter across the globe. Pretty soon, this is before I hit the next state, the whole world is a vast pile of steaming monkey's shit. But the monkey is so fuckin' greedy he starts eating himself and he shits himself through his own asshole. Then there is nothin left but monkey shit.

He's finished juicing and pours juice into the jug.

Hey! I forgot! How's the monkey?

DOLORES: Monkey's dead Hank.

HANK: Shit! Dead? Shit! Where?

DOLORES: Right here Hank, on the table.

HANK *goes to the table. He uncovers the monkey.*

HANK: Aw, hell. My little monkey!

HANK *falls on the monkey and weeps.*

DOLORES: I'm sorry Hank I'm real sorry.

HANK: My little little monkey!

DOLORES (*crying*): Broke my heart Hank, broke it right in two. I dunno what I'm gonna do without him.

HANK: Aw, my little monkey! Oh God I was gonna play so many games, I bought a bat'n ball for him, bought a big beach ball, I blew thirty-seven dollars in a kidstore . . .

DOLORES: Aw, Hank . . .

HANK: . . . gotta sackfulla nuts out there . . . big walnuts . . .

DOLORES: Hank we . . .

HANK: I think of him all the time I'm out there gunning down the freeway, can't wait to get back to my little monkey , . .

DOLORES: Can't you Hank?

HANK: My li'l monkey!

DOLORES: I loved him too Hank, he was a companion to me when you was away . . .

HANK *recovers. He straightens up and reverently replaces the blanket over the monkey's head.*

HANK: How d'e die Dolores?

DOLORES: Old age Hank.

HANK: Old age. Well. Rest in peace.

HANK *returns to the juicer. He juices more oranges.*

Any ice in the icebox?

DOLORES: I'll fix you some ice Hank.

HANK: Thank you Dolores. Mighty grateful.

DOLORES *opens the frigidaire and gets out some ice. We notice the frigidaire is empty.* DOLORES *finds a glass for HANK and places ice inside it.* HANK *fixes himself a long orange drink with a dash of vodka. He sits in the easy chair.* DOLORES *sits in a dining chair.* HANK *stares into space.* DOLORES *stares into space.*

HANK (*at length*): We're living in the armpit of an opera singer's vest Dolores. This is what I'm thinkin when I'm gunning down the freeway. We hear all round us the cacophanous overtones of a gross, distorted drama. We sense the massive shiftings of a roaring body round a stage. What we experience is stinking perspiration and the darkest corners of a dying animal in its third and final act.

DOLORES: Yes, Hank.

HANK: Yeah. It's occasions like this, when the monkey passes on, that I dream of, when I'm gunning down the freeway.

DOLORES: I know Hank.

HANK: Shit! Maybe I should ask for a new automobile.

DOLORES (*hugging* HANK): Oh Hank. I love you Hank. I love you so much!

HANK (*stroking her hair*): Thanks Dolores.

DOLORES: Hank. We've got each other now. No-one else. No monkey . . .

HANK: That's correct, Dolores . . .

DOLORES: Why don't we . . .

HANK: What?

DOLORES: Monkey around? Make love? Right here, right now, on the kitchen floor.

HANK *surveys the kitchen floor. It is filthy and covered in magazines.*

Maybe from the depths of our grief, might come, something else?

HANK: Another monkey?

DOLORES: He's up there looking down on us Hank. His spirit is with us. All around us. It'll never leave us. Maybe in ten years time we'll tell our children about the monkey and they'll say we know. We know he's here.

HANK: Say, that's a sweet thought Dolores.

DOLORES: It is Hank. I don't have many lately.

HANK: What are we doin Dolores? Shit! I'm home two goddam nights! Then it's out again. Wisconsin! Wis fuckin consin!

DOLORES: We're at a crossroads Hank.

HANK: I hate my job, my monkey's dead.

DOLORES: I was speaking with Judd a lot when you was away this trip . . .

HANK: Judd?

DOLORES: He says there's a job goin for ya anytime y'ask for it down at the junk lot . . .

HANK: I can't work for that jerk Dolores. You know that.

DOLORES: Bring you closer to me . . .

HANK: Bring me a whole lot closer to Judd . . .

DOLORES: Judd's changed. He's altered Hank, since college days . . .

HANK: How do you know?

DOLORES: I'm round there most days when you're away. Susan's my buddy, you know that.

HANK: You leave the monkey?

DOLORES: I left the monkey here Hank. I can't take him round there Hank, they have fruit trees. A date palm.

HANK: What is a jerk like that doin with a date palm?

DOLORES: What d'yexpect I should sequester myself with the monkey 24 hours a day?

HANK: Maybe that's how he died. Pining for company.

DOLORES: I never stay long Hank. I stop enough to say to Judd and Susan how much I miss you and how much I wish you'd find a job near home. That's all.

HANK: All the same . . .

DOLORES: He died of old age Hank. Please, let's not hand round blame . . .

HANK: No. No Dolores, no. If I get the smallest hint that you might've neglected my monkey, imagine what these thoughts will grow into when I'm gunning down the freeway. Shit.

DOLORES: I know how much that monkey meant to you Hank. Why the first thing y'ever did when y'walked in here was Hi monkey! Hey monkey, see what I gotcha! Out the garden monkey! Let's play ball! Oh! By the way. Hullo Dolores . . .

HANK: . . . hey . . .

DOLORES: . . . let's fuck. Scram monkey while me and Dolores fuck a little. How often d'you dream about that on the freeway huh? Because as soon as that piece of whimsy's loosed up the canal it's out agin. With hey monkey!

HANK: Dolores! Dolores! This is serious!

DOLORES: Y'know the vet said he's gotta loada fresh monkeys in the zoo right by the dolphinarium but I don't want another monkey Hank, soon as he said it I said to myself shit no. Much as I love monkeys, Hank ain't ever gonna sneak another monkey into this house. From now on, I'm Hank's monkey.

HANK: C'mon Dolores. Let's monkey.

DOLORES: I'm gonna withold monkey from you Hank, until you start out treating me like a monkey.

HANK: Ok ok ok you wanna showdown I'll give ya one . . .

He paces the room.

DOLORES: I'm not after . . .

HANK: Look at this shithole! Look at it! No food in the frigidaire! Basin fulla dishes! Magazines all over the floor! Crap all over the floor!

DOLORES: That's monkey crap!

HANK: Clean it up!

DOLORES: I spend my life cleaning up monkey shit! Soon as I've cleaned up one pile the goddam monkey goes and dumps someplace else!

HANK *lifts a magazine off the floor.*

HANK: Look at this! Monkey shit underneath the magazine!

DOLORES: That's how I clear it up Hank! I drop a magazine on it. The shit dries out and sticks to the underside of the magazine. I pick up the magazine two days later and the shit lifts clean off the floor.

HANK: Look at the magazines! Harpers and Queen! How much does that costya!

DOLORES: I don't even read the goddam magazines. I buy 'em exclusively for the shit!

HANK: So why the fuck doncha buy summin cheaper! Time magazine or Third World review!

DOLORES: The shit sticks best on glossies Hank! That's the stark facts of the world we live in . . .

HANK: C'mon Dolores. C'mon . . .

DOLORES: It cost us so much money Hank . . .

HANK: The monkey?

DOLORES: Think how much less a child would cost us. Disposable diapers. I tried diapers on the monkey once . . . I never told you. I thought you'd be offended.

HANK: What happened?

DOLORES: He ate the diaper.

HANK: Coulda bin the diaper killed him.

DOLORES: This is six years ago Hank.

HANK: Yeah, he was, getting old.

DOLORES: He was a sad old monkey Hank. Face it.

HANK: What we got t'eat?

DOLORES: Oranges.

HANK: How come we never got food?

DOLORES: Oranges are the only things the monkey wouldn't eat. I stock the frigidaire fulla food and first thing he'd do was open the door and clean it out.

HANK: Never did that when I was around . . .

DOLORES: He was a whole different animal when you was around Hank. If I tried to stop him eating he'd damn near kill me. I put a chain around the frigidaire one time and he pulled it over.

HANK: Jeez . . .

DOLORES: I kept all this from ya cus I love ya. And I know how much the monkey meant. And I know what you think about when you're gunning down the freeway. All those thoughts that crop up inside your head.

HANK: Yeah. I'm gonna put in for a new automobile Dolores. I've decided. It's the purple. Gets through to the brain.

DOLORES: Maybe something a little green. Green's relaxing.

HANK: There's a Chrysler.

DOLORES: Go for it Hank. You deserve it.

HANK: Yeh. Chrysler. Any mail?

DOLORES: Yes Hank. There's mail.

HANK: Let's see it.

DOLORE *fetches* HANK'*s mail from under a pile of Harpers. It's all the same mail. About twenty letters from the bank.*

HANK: All from the bank.

DOLORES: Yes Hank.

HANK *opens a couple of letters. Then he gives up. They contain returned checks.*

HANK: They're returning my checks now. No credit on the credit card. No cash. Nothin.

DOLORES: I have nothing either Hank.

HANK: What we gonna eat tonite?

DOLORES: Could eat the monkey Hank.

HANK: Eat the monkey?

DOLORES: The vet said it's the greatest honour we could pay him.

HANK: How the hell d'ya eat a monkey?

DOLORES: You have to skin it first.

HANK: How the hell do ya skin a monkey?

DOLORES: You cut off its extremities, nail it to the door, slit it down the middle, and yank its skin off like a coat.

HANK: Where the hell d'y learn all this?

DOLORES: Could make an orange sauce to go with it, like duck.

HANK: We could take a walk along the beach and pick seakale to go with it.

DOLORES: Oh seakale sets monkey flesh off real good . . .

HANK: It's what we stayed in California for, for Chrisssakes. The seakale and the oranges.

DOLORES: No other reason Hank. We have a banquet.

HANK: Oh Christ.

DOLORES: Cost us forty dollars to bury it.

HANK: Forty dollars? Shit. Let's eat it.

Scene Two

Three hours later.
The table is laid for two.
Candles are lit.
There is a strainer piled high with seakale and a dish of orange sauce. HANK *and* DOLORES *sit at opposite ends of the table with a plate each of roast monkey.* HANK *takes a big spoonful of kale and holds it above the strainer before he places it on the plate.*
He helps himself to orange sauce.
DOLORES *does the same.*

DOLORES: You don't know how long I've waited for this Hank.

HANK: Y'know we haven't screwed on the beach since 1980?

DOLORES: No. I know.

HANK *takes a mouthful.*
He is pleasantly surprised.

HANK: Hell this is good!

DOLORES: It's bin a lovely evening Hank.

HANK: We just left it all behind us didn't we? Takes one glorious screw on an empty beach, with the Pacific there, pounding away. I sang a song y'know?

DOLORES: Beach Boys?

HANK: You got it.

DOLORES: I thought that was what you were doing.

HANK: And now a candlelit dinner. All it

takes ain't it? What we always said. Somehow we left it all behind.

DOLORES: Just the two of us . . .

HANK: First time.

DOLORES: First time ever. First time we ever really made love, alone, without the monkey.

HANK: He was always there, on the beach, wasn't he.

DOLORES: I could never really forget him.

HANK: I just never thought, when he was alive y'know, out there in the sunshine, laughing, chattering, scratching his underarms, talking to me. He talked to me, his Daddy, my little monkey . . .

DOLORES: He talked to me too Hank.

HANK: Yeah. I know that now.

DOLORES: He talked to you through his mouth.

HANK: Used to pick the nits outa my hair . . .

DOLORES: Me too Hank.

HANK: He used to play with me Dolores did you know that? With my . . .

DOLORES: I know Hank. I know it . . .

HANK: I didn't like it much at first. Kinda disgusted me. But I thought hell it's natural. He thinks I'm his brother and that's what brother monkeys do. It's natural to a monkey. Let him fiddle around.

DOLORES: He fiddled with me too Hank.

HANK: What?

DOLORES: Oh yes. When you weren't here. He, he went a long way. He was very well-endowed Hank.

HANK: Sheeit . . .

DOLORES: Did y'ever thinka that? When you was gunnin down the freeway?

HANK: You was two-timing me with a monkey?!

DOLORES: C'mon Hank . . .

HANK: Let's have it Dolores, let's have the full story! I haven't heard the half of it have I Dolores, have I, uh! The god-dam half of it!

DOLORES: Hank you're destroying the atmosphere . . .

HANK: Me! Destroying the atmosphere ... You're a goddam cannibal! C'mon! Hit me! Give it to me straight!

DOLORES: Well first off Hank that monkey ain't the first.

HANK: The first monkey?!

DOLORES: The first shitkickin nitpickin underarm-scratching bullshit-chattering long-armed short-assed coarse-haired ape I've had the pleasure to do business with!

HANK: Business!?

DOLORES: How the fuck else d'you think I've managed to finance your goddam pet! Am I dishin y'enough dirt Hank? Uh. Food for thought? Whilst gunning down the freeway?

HANK: Stop now Dolores! Stop! Tell me it isn't true!

DOLORES: I loved that monkey Hank. First real honest male I ever came across. He didn't talk, that's the difference. That's the difference. No bullshit.

HANK: Did you used to bring 'em here? These men?

DOLORES: Oh, Hank . . .

HANK: Did ya! Dolores! Did ya! You godam bitch!

DOLORES: You couldn't give a shit about me! The monkey!

HANK: DID YA!

DOLORES: NO! I had 'em on the beach for fifteen dollars a poke!

HANK: On the beach! Fifteen dollars!

DOLORES: Then I hit on it. The big one. I had the idea some a these fat executives in their big limos might pay through the nose to watch me do it with a monkey. I was right!

HANK: Did they come here? In my house!

DOLORES: I did it in the limo! Hundred and fifty dollars! Once! Just once! Last night! Then the fuckin monkey went'n croaked on me, just when we was onto a good deal.

HANK: So that's what killed the monkey.

DOLORES: Yeah. That's what did it. That's what finally took him off.

HANK: That poor little monkey. Poor, poor goddam monkey. Old age be fucked. He just couldn't take the big time.

DOLORES: First time I ever did it on the beach Hank . . .

HANK: I'm not interested . . .

DOLORES: First time, on the beach, since 1980. I was angry.

HANK: Dolores . . .

DOLORES: . . . Angry with you, angry with the monkey, just angry I ever had to do this at all . . .

HANK: No more . . .

DOLORES: I got a guy off the street. He had a woolly hat on he never took off.

HANK: Dolores!

HANK: He forced his tongue down inside a my throat, had a tongue like a dogfish. So I bit it. He yelped and withdrew . . .

HANK: I don't believe this . . .

DOLORES: I said you wanna keep that thing on a lead . . .

HANK: You're crucifying me!

DOLORES: He said it's bin in better mouths than yours . . . I said when you've cooked it in batter and served it up with french fries you can put it back . . .

HANK: Dolores, for Chrissakes!

DOLORES: This hurting you Hank?

HANK: I'm not hearing this!

DOLORES: This hurting you more'n your goddam monkey!?

HANK: I don't hear it!

DOLORES: Well what do you wanna hear!

HANK: I wanna hear what the fuck happened to the hundred and fifty dollars!

DOLORES: Oh, Hank!

HANK: You got me doin cartwheels through a catflap here Dolores. I can't think straight.

DOLORES: D'you think thinkin straight got me into all this? D'you think I could possibly have sex with a monkey in the back of a limo with a shithead lookin at me groaning with pleasure if I was thinking straight?

HANK: Maybe you should see a shrink.

DOLORES: I don't need a shrink.

HANK: What happened to the hundred and fifty dollars?

DOLORES: The monkey ate it Hank. Last thing he ever ate.

They both remember their food, which they have almost eaten, and study what's left.

HANK: Shit.

DOLORES: Hank? Will you go see Judd?

HANK: Yeah. I'll go see Judd.

Scene Three

Two hours later.
Night.
DOLORES *sits in the easy chair. She has her head back, staring at the ceiling.* HANK *arrives home. He is very drunk. He stands unsteadily over* DOLORES.
She doesn't move.

HANK: Hi Dol.

DOLORES: See Judd?

HANK: I saw Judd.

DOLORES: What he say?

HANK: We had a few beers.

DOLORES: I can see that.

HANK: Talked over old times. Crazy y'know. Crazy. When y'ole buddy, he's sitting there, in his chair, he said to me y'know Hank, we're livin in the crutch of a ballerina's tut . . .

DOLORES: He did?

HANK: He went on to tell me exactly the thoughts I'd had whilst gunning down the freeway. He put it more er . . .

DOLORES: Elegiacally.

HANK: Yeah.

DOLORES: 'Comes a sitting in a junkyard.

HANK: He always had this gift . . .

DOLORES: What else you talk about?

HANK: I was saying, phyaw, shit. Crazy. Crazy y'know. Crazy. Only takes two buddies sitting in a junklot. Talkin over old times . . . This is it. Old times. Christ we went through it with a toothcomb Dolores. Chicago, high school, college, his dad, my dad, his ma, my ma, the autos we had, the surfing, the monkey, Mexico . . .

DOLORES: . . . covered a lotta ground.

HANK: Two buddies. Sitting in a junklot. Talkin over old times. Rakin up the past. Dredgin it up. Spreading the shit. Few beers. We was watchin the waves. There was a pointbreak out there . . .

DOLORES: Always was . . .

HANK: Shit the waves was, musta bin six foot. Perfect shape. I said you still surf Judd? He said yeah. Still surf. Just like that. Yeah. That hurt. That hurt me. How could the bastard be so fuckin cruel?

DOLORES: Y'expect him to lie and say no?

HANK: It was the least he could do!

DOLORES: You asked him!

HANK: Yeah. Guess so.

He can't stand any more. He lies on the floor.

DOLORES: Say anything else?

HANK: We reminisced. We raked up the past, no stone unturned Dol . . .

DOLORES: Yeah you said that . . .

HANK: I'm making my point.

DOLORES: Well make it before you forget it.

HANK: We ain't got nowhere Judd, er Dolores. We ain't got nothing. And it takes, it takes a, it takes a goddam history! History lesson to bring it on home to this little brain a mine, that the country is a monkey's asshole . . .

DOLORES: No more dime-store philosophy Hank . . .

HANK: This ain't, this is the real thing . . .

DOLORES: New start Hank . . .

HANK: This country . . .

DOLORES: No Hank!

HANK: Hear me OUT! Blast ya! Hear what I have to say! This is important! To me!

DOLORES: Go ahead Hank.

HANK: It . . . it's . . . just . . . I forgot.

DOLORES: Doesn't matter does it. What you think. It's what you do. Did ya talk about that? The future?

HANK: Hell no Dolores. We was so wrapped up in the past we clean forgot to talk about the future.

DOLORES: So you never got round to talkin about workin for him.

HANK: The guy's a jerk Dolores.

DOLORES: A jerk.

HANK: I can't work with a jerk. Honest. I can't.

DOLORES: He ain't jerk enough for you to drink his beer.

HANK: Shit I take beer off any bastard. I have to.

DOLORES: How come he's a jerk? So you can't work with the guy.

HANK: I didn't say I can't work with the guy.

DOLORES: Sure you did . . .

HANK: Said I can't work with a jerk.

DOLORES: You called him a jerk. So you can't work with the guy.

HANK: That's exactly what *I* said. You know me Dolores. I'd be impossible to live with.

He shuts his eyes. It's too much to shut them, so he opens them again. He sleeps with his eyes open, staring at the stars.

DOLORES: Y'know I knew a guy once Hank.

HANK: Yeah?

DOLORES: He was a great guy.

HANK: Yeah.

DOLORES: He had a beat up Oldsmobile, with a surfboard on top. Kinda surfboard you don't see no more. It was a seven foot six surfboard, with one fin. Kinda surfboard if ya put it on top of a beat up

Oldsmobile it turns a few heads, when he was gunning down Main street. Shit could he ride that board this guy. He was poetry to watch. He could hang five, hang ten, quasimodo, head dip, shoot the tube, he didn't talk about it, he did it. He couldn't give a shit about the world or the country or nothin. He'd bin to college but he was no buck-chaser. And y'know what about this guy? Y'know what it was that set him up above all the thousand other guys just like him? For me? What did it for me, was this guy had a monkey. A sweet, good-natured, springy li'l monkey. Monkey went everywhere with this guy. Slept with him, walked with him, ate with him, talked with him. He surfed with him! I remember when they held the world championships, right here on this beach, Micky Pentz, from Hawaii, the world champion and everybody's god, asked to surf with the monkey for his sponsor, and he couldn't do it. He wiped out and almost drowned the monkey. There was only one guy who could hang five with a monkey on his back, cus he was the only one guy in the whole fuckin world who couldn't give a shit about anything else except hanging five with a monkey on his back! Micky Pentz tried it for his sponsor, earn hisself a few extra bucks! He didn't do it for the monkey! And he wiped out! There was only one guy Hank! Y'know who that was Hank? Y'know who that was!

HANK: No?

DOLORES: It was you Hank! It was you! Did you talk with Judd about that? Did you talk about that? Did it hurt too much to talk about that? Did you think about it? Did you ever think about that when you was gunning down the freeway Hank?

HANK: We can get a fresh monkey . . .

DOLORES: I don't wanna fresh monkey! I wanna fresh Hank!

HANK: You want the old Hank. You ain't gonna get the old Hank.

DOLORES: I don't want the old Hank. I said, I wanna fresh Hank! A new Hank. A future Hank! But I want that little essence, of the old Hank, somewhere in the new Hank! Its still there, somewhere Hank, but it's bin smothered with shit. Now I'm prepared to dig around a little

bit Hank, and find it, but I need you here, with me. Cus right now I see you three days a month then you're off again down the freeway and filling your head with shit. So if you go off again in two days time to Wisconsin, you take me with you, or you leave me behind. But I won't be here when you get back.

Silence.
DOLORES *puts her head back and stares at the ceiling.*

DOLORES: You throw up tonite Hank?

Hank is asleep. She kicks him where she sits.

DOLORES: Hank!

HANK *wakes up.*

DOLORES: You were asleep?

HANK: Guess so.

DOLORES: When did you fall asleep?

HANK: Hell I dunno. Right about the last time you mentioned the monkey.

DOLORES: When was that Hank?

HANK *grunts.*

DOLORES: You throw up tonite Hank?

HANK: Uh?

DOLORES: You throw up tonite?

DOLORES: I think I'm about to. The stars are spinning round.

DOLORES: We're inside Hank.

HANK: Then I'm about to.

He gets up and runs out back.
DOLORES *sets her head back and stares at the ceiling.*

Scene Four

Next Day.
Morning.
HANK *is on the phone. He's reached the end of a conversation. He slams the phone down and whoops for joy.*

HANK: Hay Dolores! Dolores! Hear this!

DOLORES' *voice comes from out back. It's indecipherable.*

HANK: Come out here! Come right out here!

DOLORES *enters. She is in a dressing-gown.*

HANK: This is the big one honey! This is where our fortunes change! They got me selling bibles in Nebraska! Y'know the last guy who did that? George Nitscratchski? He cleared twenny-four hundred dollars in three days! They love me. They love me. Someone in that pool loves me! They only ever give that pitch to a man who's earned it right? Dolores, this is it!

DOLORES: When do they want ya?

HANK: Right now. Jeff Lonsdale, sent him up there for er, harvest thanksgiving, that's a big time for bibles, right? He's had a heart attack. Whizzkid, he was only twenny-six, needs a replacement right away or they miss the, the . . .

DOLORES: So you're going now huh?

HANK: This minute. Seeya honey. Back in one month a rich man . . .

DOLORES: I won't be here Hank . . .

HANK: Yeah yeah OK, OK. Seeya.

DOLORES: You won't Hank.

HANK: I'll get a sub from the pool right? Three hundred dollars. Send it down to you . . .

DOLORES: It'll pay for my fare.

HANK: Where the fuck to? C'mon Dolores they want me now . . .

DOLORES: Then go.

HANK: You're screwing me up! Fuck what is this?! You're screwin me up!

DOLORES: Goodbye Hank . . .

HANK: My finest hour! You're screwin it up!

DOLORES: I'm not Hank . . .

HANK: You're shittin on me! You don't want the money? You don't wannit!? Christ, you're perverse! You're a crazy bitch! You be here right! You be here when I get back! You be here when I get back or I'll never see y'again! I'll walk out on ya!

DOLORES: You walk out here now and you walk out on me cus I won't be here when you get back to walk out on! And yes, you will never see me again. Ever ever.

HANK: Goodbye Dolores!

He walks out into the garden. He stops.

HANK: Shit. C'mon c'mon c'mon c'mon . . .

DOLORES: C'mon Hank. It's my ultimatum I'm afraid.

HANK: I can't . . .

DOLORES: Take me with you . . .

HANK: I can't take you with me. No women no blacks, y'know the rules.

DOLORES: Goodbye Hank.

Hank comes back. He holds Dolores.

HANK: You be here huh? You be here please? Please honey, you be here? Please?

He drops to his knees and holds her round the waist, sobbing.

DOLORES: I will not.

HANK: I forgived ya for all that with the monkey. I forgived ya for all that with the monkey. I forgived ya didn't I?

DOLORES: There was nothing to forgive.

HANK: Start out again, fresh start, new hopes, big money Dolores. Shit we spoke all that. Two days, non-stop, great, heroic talk . . .

DOLORES: All for nothing Hank, if you go through that gate.

HANK: I gotta go through the gate. I got to!

DOLORES: Go Hank. Look at me. Look at my face.

HANK *looks up at* DOLORES' *face with tearfilled eyes.* DOLORES' *eyes are dry. She is cool.*

DOLORES: Look at my face. No tears. No nothing. I don't care Hank. It's your choice. Go or stay, I don't mind. But I don't care either way. I don't care.

HANK: Y'ain't cryin?

DOLORES: I ain't cryin.

HANK: You don't care?

DOLORES: It's what I said. I don't care. One day we might meet again, in a limousine. Green Chrysler perhaps.

You'll be fat and successful, and I'll be laid out in the back, screwin a monkey.

HANK: Shit no.

DOLORES: You know what I'll be seeing? With my eyes shut? A lovely guy, hanging five, with a monkey on his back. He's the guy who'll make me cry. He's the guy who'll make me care. Not you Hank.

HANK: I don't know what you're talkin about . . .

DOLORES: You don't Hank, cus you were asleep.

HANK: Who the fuck is this guy, while I was asleep?

DOLORES: It was you Hank.

HANK *rises*

HANK (*indignant*): While I was asleep?!

DOLORES: You weren't asleep for all of it Hank. But you weren't listening, or you didn't comprehend, or whatever, it doesn't matter does it.

HANK*'s bag is waiting for him. He picks it up and heads for the garden gate. The* VET *appears through the gate. He carries a hutch. It is heavy with the weight of an animal. Unseen.*

VET: Hi there.

HANK: Who the hell's this?

DOLORES: Oh! Hullo. This is the, er, vet Hank.

VET: Mrs Wandaback. Mr Wandaback, I'm glad to find you home.

HANK Yeah I'm glad to find me home. (*to Dolores*): He don't look like a vet to me.

VET: Mr Wandaback I'm a vet. Believe me I'm a vet. And I'm a vet with glad tidings for you people here today.

DOLORES: We owe him some money Hank. Sixty cents.

HANK: Here . . .

VET: No. Mr Wandaback let me say first how sorry I was to be the one who had to proclaim your monkey dead. But I've found in the past if an animal's dead there's no point saying otherwise.

HANK: I can understand that.

VET: Thank you sir.

HANK: You're welcome.

VET: Sir I got to thinking after I left this household how poignant was the reaction of your good wife. Most times, when an animal grows old like yours, particularly a monkey, there is a sense of relief. With Mrs Wandaback it was different. Here was real devotion. How truly sad she seemed. How selfless. How she thought of you and how you would take it. How bereft you would be. Got to thinking here was a couple who worshipped their pet. Who cared for their pet like a child. No sooner had I arrived back at the zoo, when I was called upon to administer to a birth. What my job's all about Mr Wandaback. Birth and death. And what's in between. Disease. But never has the juxtaposition between birth and death been so vivid. Never have I left a scene so heavy with grief, and after a short journey in my car, why as you know, you take a right outa here, straight down Main street, left at the bank, and there's the zoo, right between the high school and the DA's office. I hopped from my car and was overwhelmed with all the joyous grunts and moans of, of motherhood. I gazed down at the helpless, newborn litter, and one little fellow turned his blind eyes at me and made the soft, mewling cry which is the hallmark of all animals at that point in their lives when the world is an innocent place, devoid of evil. And I thought to myself, you gorgeous little beasty. You defenceless, wise pathetic little goobydoobywooby-noonoo. You deserve better than a zoo. I'll try you out on the Wandabacks. They will take you to their bosom. They will feed you, and nurture you, and, and love, yes love you. I've brought it with me. In its very own little hutch. Please, please, take it, please.

HANK: What is it?

DOLORES (*in tears*): Its a goobydoobywoobynoonoo Hank. Weren't you listening?

VET: Oh no Mrs Wandaback. Bless you. That's my personal way of talking to animals, it seems to get results. No this is a, a very rare breed of, now don't be put off, it's nothing like the kind you eat. Its a Macedonian Curly Pig. Take a look.

HANK *and* DOLORES *look inside the hutch.*

DOLORES: Oh. It's beautiful.

HANK: Little whopper.

VET: They don't grow a whole lot.

HANK: Is it a boar or a girl?

VET: Its a, a, er, boar.

HANK: That's good.

DOLORES: A little boar. Oh, Hank.

HANK: Whaddathey eat?

VET: Oh, er anything. Anything at all you care to throw at 'em. Except pork.

HANK: Respond to training?

VET: Oh yes. Train 'em. They have a very high intelligence rating. There's some states accept 'em as dogs in their canine shows . . .

DOLORES: Oh . . .

VET: You can do 'em up real nice, train their curls to go one way with rollers? I saw one with a pearl bracelet through its nose and eiffel tower earrings. Won a big rosette in the poodle section.

DOLORES: Oh, Hank . . .

HANK: Certainly tugs at my heartstrings Dolores . . .

DOLORES: Mine too Hank. Mine too.

HANK: You ah, you reckon I could take it surfing with me?

DOLORES (*ecstatic*): Oh! Hank!

HANK: If I made a backpouch for it, slung it on my back.

VET: See no reason why not. They take to water. They're like ducks in water. Quite amphibious.

HANK: Like a dog on land, like a duck in water. Could call it Dogduck.

DOLORES: Dogduck.

VET: Dolores, Hank, and Dogduck.

HANK *bends and takes a look in the hutch.*

HANK: Dogduck. Hey Dogduck, (*whistles.*) Here boy, Dogduck. Dogduck . . . Hey he knows his name. Dogduck. He's a bright boy. Ch'choo . . .

DOLORES *joins* HANK *at the hutch.*

DOLORES: Dogduck? Hey, Dogduck? Good firm teech Hank he's got.

HANK: What is he snarling or grinning?

DOLORES: Oh he's smiling Hank you can see that. He's so sweet.

HANK: Hey Dogduck. Responded that time y'see that?

DOLORES: We could manicure his, his tusks Hank, make them less sharp . . .

The VET *heaves a sigh of relief and starts to slope off, leaving* HANK *and* DOLORES *cooing over Dogduck. They continue cooing over Dogduck as the lights fade.*

ACT TWO

Scene One

Six months later.
The room is cleared and brighter.
Effort has been made to make the place more nest-like. A Malibu board stands outside.
DOLORES is slumped downstage in the easy chair. She wears beachwear, she is wet and bedraggled. The VET stands by the table, he is wet through and dripping. Around the table, on the chairs and the floor, are candelabra, cutlery, glasses and mats, hastily removed from the table in the crisis.
HANK lies unconscious on the table. He is covered to the waist with the Indian blanket. His chest is exposed and the VET examines him with his stethoscope.
The VET ceases his examination, and after opening HANK's mouth and peering down his throat, walks down to DOLORES.

DOLORES: Is he dead?

VET: Hell no. He's gonna be dandy.

DOLORES: You're a very brave man.

VET: Please, no.

DOLORES: You risked your life. You charged into the sea and dragged him unconscious through the boiling surf. You laid him on the sand and resuscitated him, God knows how . . .

VET: Mouth to mouth. Never pleasant.

DOLORES: You literally grasped him back from the jaws of hell. I don't know how to repay you.

VET: Bless you Mrs Wandaback, I'll overlook the fee.

DOLORES: What about Dogduck?

VET: Leave Dogduck to me. He'll be capering on the beach. Your husband has had a traumatic time. He needs rest, attention, love and understanding.

DOLORES: What should I do when he comes through?

VET: Do you know anything about seaweed Mrs Wandaback?

DOLORES: We practically live off the soup.

VET: First thing you do with a drowning victim is check his oesophagus and trachea for debris, such as weed, which might impair his breathing. You ah, you're familiar with the dark brown, slimy stuff I'm sure, with the little pods full of air? Ones we used to squeeze between our fingernails when we was kids and pop!

DOLORES: Oh of course! I know the ones! We did that a whole lot! It was fun.

VET: I still do it.

DOLORES: So do I, when no-one's looking.

VET: I did it to your husband's tonsils.

DOLORES: O my God.

VET: They're a touch inflamed that's all. He may feel a little hoarse. Hot milk.

DOLORES: I'll warm some.

VET: Lace it with honey.

DOLORES: I'm sure he'd love Dogduck to be here when he . . .

VET: I'll go after him now . . .

DOLORES: I hope you find him, for Hank's sake.

VET: I surely will.

DOLORES: Hank loves him so much.

VET: I can see that.

DOLORES: You can?

VET: I felt privileged when he invited me along today, to such a touching event. I'm only sad it had to end like it did.

DOLORES: I just dunno what I woulda done if he'd, if he'd drowned.

VET: They are tenacious beasts, and natural swimmers.

DOLORES: No I . . . oh . . .

She buries her head in her hands. HANK grunts and stirs. DOLORES rushes to him and smothers him.

DOLORES: Hank! Oh Hank!

HANK: Dolores. That you?

DOLORES: It's me Hank.

HANK: What the fuck happenned?

DOLORES: You wiped out Hank! You wiped out!

HANK: Dogduck?

VET: Dogduck's gonna be fine Mr Wandaback.

HANK *grips his throat.*

HANK: Uygh! My throat!

VET: Your lymphatic tissue will be tender for a while Mr Wandaback. I was a touch zealous, in the heat of the moment. I waived the fee.

HANK: What the fuck did you do?

DOLORES: He saved your life honey, that's what he did.

VET: I'll, er . . .

HANK: Saved my life! I wiped out, that's all! It's when he grabbed me I lost consciousness!

DOLORES: Oh Hank, it wasn't like that Sweetpea . . .

HANK: Dolores!

He chokes.

HANK: My throat! What the fuck did ya do to my throat!

DOLORES: Hank!

VET: He's traumatised!

DOLORES: You took a bad wipe out! We saw from the beach, we were there Hank! Now if the vet hadn't waded in and pulled y'out who knows how it woulda turned out Hank! for Chrissakes he saved your life!

HANK: What the fuck did he do to my throat!

DOLORES: He pinched your goddam tonsils that's all!

HANK: I don't have any fuckin tonsils!

VET (*sloping off*): I'd better dash . . .

HANK: Scram before I rip your tongue out!

DOLORES (*to the vet*): Thank you so much. Thank you.

VET: Remember. Love and under-standing.

DOLORES: Hot milk.

The VET *goes.*

HANK: Feel like I gone ten rounds with the Boston Strangler . . .

DOLORES: I'm supposed to give you love

and understanding Hank, because you've had a traumatic experience.

HANK *chokes badly.* DOLORES *panics.*

DOLORES: O my God! Hank? Milk!

She runs towards the kitchenette. HANK, *choking, makes noises and points at his back.* DOLORES *comes and hits him hard on the back.* HANK *throws his hands to his mouth and regurgitates violently. From the recesses of his mouth he withdraws a small sprig of seaweed.*

HANK: Gimme a glass of water.

DOLORES *does this.* HANK *takes the glass and drops the seaweed in it.*

HANK: Evidence.

DOLORES: Have you any idea what it costs for a qualified medical person to save your life here in California? He did it for nothing!

HANK: I wouldn't speak too soon if I were you, my throat is killing me.

DOLORES: It's tender that's all. It'll clear up in time. Honeybunch?

HANK: Yeah. Guess so.

DOLORES: Come on.

HANK: OK. Dolores?

DOLORES: Yes Hank?

HANK: I'm sorry.

DOLORES: That's fine.

HANK: I'm sorry I fucked up. Hell I'm so sorry. I'm sorry Dolores I'm so sorry I fouled up.

DOLORES: Hank. Sweetpea. You are older than you once were.

DOLORES *caresses* HANK.

HANK: Its bin a wonderful six months Dolores.

DOLORES: Yes Hank.

HANK: The days on the beach. You me and the pig. They were golden days weren't they?

DOLORES: Yes.

HANK: All the hours we spent planning for today. The day, the date, the hour, the minute when I would rise again with

Dogduck on my back, slung in a backpouch riding a perfect perfect six foot pointbreak up to fuckin heaven! The motto, remember the motto you dreamed up?

DOLORES: Old surfers never die.

HANK: Old surfers never die . . . they drown!

DOLORES: Oh Hank . . .

HANK: I'm sorry kid . . .

DOLORES: Please don't be melancholy . . .

HANK *is in tears.*

DOLORES: I'll fix you some milk.

DOLORES *goes to the kitchenette and puts the milk on.* HANK *struggles off the table, wrapped in the Indian blanket. He feels his throat and hobbles to the fridge. The fridge is empty except for one can of beer. He takes the beer, shuts the fridge and hobbles to the easy chair. He sits and opens the beer. He drinks and places the can on the floor.*

HANK: Dolores.

DOLORES (*in the kichenette*): What is it honey?

HANK: I love you Dolores.

DOLORES: I love you too.

HANK: Ya. Good.

He takes a drink of beer while DOLORES *is tinkering in the kitchenette.*

HANK: What are you doin?

DOLORES: Oh, tinkering.

HANK: In the kitchenette?

DOLORES: Heating some milk.

HANK: Why don't we monkey around uh?

DOLORES: You want to?

HANK: Heck I'm hot if you are.

DOLORES: I'll lie back and let you do it to me Hank.

DOLORES *has entered from the kitchenette and is re-setting the table.*

HANK: I love you Dolores.

DOLORES: I'll get into it as we progress.

HANK: Doesn't make you feel horny. Fact that I'm horny.

DOLORES: Oh sure it does Hank.

HANK: Then why lie back and let me do it?

DOLORES: I said, I'd get into it.

HANK: If you're already horny Dolores, what's keeping you?

DOLORES: You're splitting hairs Hank.

HANK: I don't think so.

DOLORES: Alright. You lie back and I'll go on top.

HANK: I'm happy on top.

DOLORES: I'd prefer to go on top.

HANK: Why's that?

DOLORES: Whichever you like Hank.

HANK: Because if you lie back and I go on top my gut hangs down is that it?

DOLORES: Hank. You don't have a gut.

HANK: I have a gut. Don't kid me I don't have a gut.

DOLORES: It may take a little longer for me to get into it if I lie back. It might have to do with your non-existent gut, or the paint on the ceiling which is flaking . . .

HANK: There.

DOLORES: Whatever Hank, perhaps I'm just the kinda girl who likes to fuck on top.

HANK: You fucked every whichway in the past, when I didn't have a gut.

DOLORES: Why don't we just forget it?

HANK: It was on the agenda!

DOLORES *has poured hot milk into a jug and brought it round to* HANK.

DOLORES: You don't want this.

HANK: I don't?

DOLORES: You got yourself a beer.

HANK: Then I won't have the milk.

DOLORES: You're supposed to drink the milk.

HANK: You just told me I didn't want it.

DOLORES: With beer? I've heard of mixing your drinks Hank.

HANK: You have the beer. It's our last beer. I'll drink the milk.

DOLORES: I don't want the beer. I don't drink beer. I'm watching my weight.

HANK: What is that supposed to mean?

DOLORES: Means I don't want the beer Hank.

HANK: Means you're beating me round the head with my gut.

DOLORES: I'm not beating you round the head with your gut Hank. You are.

HANK: Well your jugs are in great shape if that's any consolation.

DOLORES: I don't recall I was seeking any.

HANK: I was?

DOLORES: No Hank. No. Thank you for paying me the compliment about my breasts.

HANK: And your butt has never looked better.

DOLORES: My butt is spreading. I had to let out my beachwear.

HANK: That's exactly what I mean. I always thought you had a too-slender butt. It's a well-proportioned butt now. The cheeks jostle when you walk. That's how I like it.

DOLORES: Then perhaps I should lie on my stomach.

HANK: I'm not the problem.

DOLORES: I never said I was. I said I was happy to lay back and let you do it Hank.

HANK: Well for fucksake then let's!

DOLORES: No! I'm sorry Hank. I'm not in the mood.

DOLORES *takes the milk back to the kitchenette.* HANK *drinks his beer. The* VET *enters.*

VET: Am I interrupting anything?

HANK: No!

DOLORES: Is it Dogduck?

VET: Yes.

HANK: What.

VET: He stayed in the sea some time after our evacuation of the beach. Then he came out of the water and frolicked on the sand. He was sportsome and I couldn't catch him. Do you know Mrs Operkl?

HANK: Yes! We know Mrs Operkl.

VET: She was walking her dog down the far end of the beach. A big dalmatian, named Spotty. Dogduck scampered up to Spotty and rolled on his back, begging for his tummy to be tickled and licked. Spotty severed his spinal cord, dislocating the odontoid peg and punctured the trachea, with his teeth.

HANK: Say that again?

VET: Spotty bit off Dogduck's head.

This sinks deep in HANK.

DOLORES: Is he dead?

HANK: Awwwww, SHIT!

VET: He was snorting and slavering with glee right up to the last Mrs Wandaback. He died a happy pig.

HANK: Dead! Dead!

DOLORES: Don't blame yourself Hank.

HANK: Who the fuck does she think she is she can allow her dog to do a thing like that!

DOLORES: Dogs do this Hank they're a . . .

HANK: What the hell kinda beach is it you can't allow an innocent pig to run around without having his fuckin head bit off!

DOLORES: Hank, please, don't get heated . . .

HANK: These fuckin widows they retire down here on their ole man's life insurance and they havn't bin here five minutes they think they own the fuckin place!

DOLORES: This is not the case Hank.

HANK: I won't have it!

DOLORES: Neither will I Hank now wrap up!

HANK: I held down a rotten fuckin job for fifteen years Dolores and I have citizen's rights like any other bastard!

DOLORES: No you don't Hank.

HANK: And if I say my pig can caper down

a beach there ain't no fuckin Operkl in the whole of the United States gonna deny me that right!

DOLORES: *She* didn't bite his head off Hank, her *dog* did!

HANK: I will not be intimidated!

DOLORES: Nobody's intimidating you!

HANK: Operkl's intimidating me!

DOLORES: Her dog bit your pig's head off, that's all!

HANK: That's not intimidation?!

DOLORES: No!

VET: It's a species typical posture . . .

HANK: Who's next Dolores? Who's safe on that beach now?

VET: The dog is being treated in our psychiatric unit, right by the elephant compound.

HANK: Dogduck one day, me the next, that's the way I see it Dolores, and that is intimidation!

VET: We identify the stimulii, then we de-sensitise him and counter-condition his responses.

DOLORES (*indicating* HANK): Whose, his?

VET: The dog's to pigs.

HANK: Shoot him! For Chrissakes shoot him!

VET: That is a premature reaction if I may say so Mr Wandaback . . .

HANK: Premature!?

DOLORES: It's prehistoric!

HANK: Who's fuckin side are you on!

VET: Counter-conditioning is a long and expensive process, but Mrs Operkl can afford it and the results can be astonishing. Everyone is rewarded, Mrs Operkl, her dog, me, and of course, pigs.

HANK: Those who still have a head!

DOLORES: Hank!

HANK: And I haven't noticed you so fuckin sorry to see the back of it!

DOLORES: Back of what?

HANK: His head!

DOLORES: That's right! That's right! That's right Hank I hated him!

HANK: You hated him?

DOLORES: Dogduck was not the answer Hank.

HANK: You, you gave him everything.

DOLORES: I don't need reminding of that.

HANK: You hated him?

DOLORES: I despised him.

HANK: You devoted six months of your life to him.

DOLORES: Not to him Hank, to you.

HANK: Spent our last nickel on him.

DOLORES: You did. Prime steaks, sweet potatoes, he ate more'n the goddam monkey!

HANK: Gave him a little bell to hang round his neck at Thanksgiving . . .

DOLORES: Tinkle tinkle drove me up the goddam wall!

HANK: You was up all nite knitting him a lounge-coat!

DOLORES: Which he never wore!

HANK: Yes he did Dolores he wore it round the house with his bootees.

DOLORES: He wore the Easter bonnet with his bootees Hank whilst unpicking the lounge-coat with his tusks!

HANK: You hated him? You hated him? You hated him?

DOLORES: Yes. Hank. I hated him.

HANK: Aw shit! How can you say that?

DOLORES: Because I'm through with lying. We've had six months of lies Hank. You can't change back to what you were. You are what you are now and I . . . I despise it.

HANK: Despise what?

DOLORES: You Hank.

HANK: Me too?

DOLORES: Yes. You too.

HANK: Aw hell!

DOLORES: I force myself to like it and *I*

change. *I* become dishonest. Then we're both liars Hank. Trying to kid each other we're telling the truth. We know we're not telling the truth but we believe each other's lies. After that its meltdown. We lie and we lie and we lie and we lie and we go down and down and down. Then we patch up and up and up and we look down the chasm and all the patches are there, bulging with lies. There's nothing there any more Hank.

HANK *is stunned.*

HANK (*to the* VET): I gave up my job for this! I could've had Nebraska now! I could be a wealthy man! I gave it all up for this! And I went out there, struggling with the ocean for the day I surfed with Dogduck on my back and all the time she was sitting here on her fat butt hating him!

DOLORES: My FAT BUTT!

HANK: And despising me!

DOLORES: I've done everything I can . . .

HANK: You've done everything, you've done nothin! The only thing you done is lay out in the back of a limousine and . . .

DOLORES (*screams*): No!!!!

HANK: . . . get fucked by a monkey!

Silence. DOLORES *turns to ice. The* VET *colours.*

VET (*at length*): Mrs . . .

DOLORES (*seething*): Gettout.

The VET *sidles, reluctantly, off.*

DOLORES: How can you say that? In front of a vet!

HANK: Did he go on top? Did his fuckin gut hang down?

DOLORES: That's digusting. That is truly disgusting.

HANK: The great advantage of an aging monkey. They manage to keep a concave gut.

The VET *returns*

VET: Mrs Wandaback? Is is true? I have to know.

DOLORES: Yes. It is true.

VET: In the back of a limo?

DOLORES: Yes.

VET: By day? Or nite?

DOLORES: It was dark. I had my eyes shut.

VET: Was the courtesy light on?

DOLORES: How in hell should I know!

VET: It's astounding.

DOLORES: It's disgusting!

VET: Mrs Wandaback I can't tell you how excited I am by these revelations. Intimacy with a monkey. We've been trying to achieve this for years! Your rapport with animals is, is unique. Did you know the Macedonian Curly pig has been known to disembowel cattle? The MCP is one of the most alienation – sensitive creatures known to vets, and yet you, whilst apparently hating Dogduck, managed to bring him up a docile, fun-loving creature who wore an easter bonnet, bootees, and unpicked a woollen lounge coat with his tusks! Mrs Wandaback . . .

HANK: Hey mister willya get the hell outa here before I bite your goddam head off!

VET: Sir I have to speak with your wife.

DOLORES: Let him have his say Hank, now you've told him.

VET: Mrs Wandaback, under article three of the constitution of our zoo we are required to maintain a comprehensive remedial unit. Ours operates on a range of fronts from basic animal psycho-therapy at $40 an hour right up to the very frontiers of neurological research which is funded by the Pentagon. The spearhead of our programme right now is an in-depth study of species-typical behaviourisms which is being conducted by me and Artie Kake, the giraffe steward. Mrs Wandaback, we want you on our team. Come and join us? I mentioned we received generous patronage from the military, we could pay you in telephone numbers.

DOLORES: To fuck monkeys?

VET: Oh no! Bless you, no. Just to be there. Just to sit with unsettled animals, and be one of them.

DOLORES *says nothing.* HANK *scowls.*

VET: Think it over. But remember you are a very remarkable person. You should consider the benefits you could bring to the animal kingdom, the whole human race, and perhaps above all, me and Artie Kake.

The VET *goes. After a while,* DOLORES *speaks.*

DOLORES: I'll never forgive you for this.

HANK: You put me there. You drove me to it.

DOLORES: I did no such thing. I told the truth. That's all. I told the truth.

HANK: You gonna take this job?

DOLORES: Of course I will.

HANK: And leave me?

DOLORES: Who knows where your jealousy and envy will stop? You bring out our dirtiest linen and wash it in front of a vet.

HANK: You gonna leave me here? On my own? All day?

DOLORES: It'll get me out of the house Hank. Could be the one hope I have left to preserve my sanity.

HANK: That's the first thing you'll lose working with a guy like that! He's a lunatic! He can't tell an airpod from a fuckin tonsil! Who the fuck ever psycho-analysed a dog?! It's no accident he works in a zoo Dolores, what beats me is they let him out!

DOLORES: Do you think I don't know a nutcase when I see one Hank?

HANK: What's more he's a jerk.

DOLORES: Oh that too.

HANK: Then don't take the job.

DOLORES: Oh no Hank. I'll take the job. I'll grab the job by the neck and rattle its bones, you see if I don't.

Scene Two

Several days later.
The shack is empty
HANK *enters, running.*
He wears shorts, tee-shirt, a towel round his neck, and running pumps. He puts his hands on the table ledge and leans forward, panting. He takes the towel from round his

neck and wipes his face and neck. He straightens up and feels his gut for firmness. He looks down at his gut and takes a fold of flesh in his hands and squeezes it. He flings his hands in the air and places them round the back of his head.
Legs apart, he bends sharply to touch his knee with the opposite elbow.
Hits the table with his elbow.
Yelps with pain and hugs his elbow.
Removes his pumps and stockings.
Leaps onto the table.
He shoves cutlery, etc. to one end of the table with his bare foot.
Kneels at the other end of the table and faces out.
Paddles furiously with his arms down either side of the table.
Grunts as he's doing this.
Suddenly jumps to his feet and establishes a surfing stance.
Surfs the table.
Checks his gut from time to time as he twists and bends his body.
Checks his watch.
Starts 'Walking the Board'.
Walks up to the front edge of the table and hangs five toes over the edge of the table.
Twists and leaps in the air.
Lands on a fork. Yelps, grabs his foot, hopping on the other.
Falls off the table. He sits on the floor nursing his elbow, foot and butt.

HANK: SHIT!

DOLORES *enters.*
She carries two brown bags of groceries.
She is dressed smart in expensive clothes.
She walks to the table.
Sets the groceries down in the space HANK *cleared for his surfing.*
Takes a glossy magazine from one bag and crosses to the easy chair.
Kicks off her shoes and reads the magazine.
HANK *rises painfully to his feet.*
Curls his injured foot and walks with a limp.
He unpacks the groceries from the bags. They contain expensive items of food. Two steaks, wrapped, HANK *leaves on the table, along with a clove of garlic.*
He limps to the fridge with beer, wine, champagne and oranges.
He takes a huge bunch of grapes and cookies into the kitchenette.
DOLORES *reads her magazine.*
HANK *emerges, limping, from the*

kitchenette.
He carries the grapes, washed, in a bowl.
He sets the bowl down beside
DOLORES.
DOLORES *reads and eats grapes,*
absently.
HANK *carries more groceries through to*
the kitchenette.
DOLORES *reads and eats grapes.*
HANK *limps from the kitchenette with a*
chopping board, garlic crusher and steak
hammer.
Unwraps the steaks and crushes the garlic.
Rubs the garlic into the steaks.
Beats the steaks mercilessly with the
hammer.
Exhausted, he sits back.
DOLORES *reads and eats grapes.*
HANK *engages her in disjointed*
conversation.

HANK: You're late back from work.

DOLORES (*reading*): Yes.

HANK: Where you bin?

DOLORES: I called by on Susan.

HANK *stands and grabs a steak in each*
hand. Slides them off the chopping board
and dangles them by his sides. Limps out
with them to the kitchenette.
DOLORES *reads and eats grapes.*
HANK *emerges from the kitchenette*
wearing an apron. The apron is tied tight at
the back. HANK *wipes his hands on the*
apron, over his gut. This draws attention
to his shape again.

HANK: What did you do today. At the
zoo?

HANK *finds a mirror hanging on the wall*
and removes it. Sets it up on a chair so he
can see his body-profile. As he speaks he
checks his stance, with the apron on.
DOLORES *eats grapes and reads as she*
speaks.

DOLORES: I sat up a tree talking to a
giraffe.

HANK: Say anything interesting?

DOLORES: I didn't mention your name
Hank, if that's what you mean.

HANK: Was he eating?

DOLORES: Yes.

HANK: Wanna be careful they don't bite
your head off. They got vicious teeth.

DOLORES: This giraffe doesn't have any.

HANK: A giraffe with no teeth?

DOLORES: He's a radiation victim.
Military stuff.

HANK *has discovered his gut protrudes*
less the looser the apron is tied. He
experiments with stance-related string
tensions.

DOLORES: We had an airforce colonel
visit the unit today. He was impressed
with our progress. Gonna designate us
more funds. Means I get a raise.

DOLORES *has eaten her last grape.*
HANK *heads for the kitchenette.*

DOLORES: He gave up eating.

HANK: That's terminal.

HANK *is in the kitchenette.* DOLORES
reads and picks grape skin from her teeth.

DOLORES: The only way they could get it
eating again was to put me up a tree along
with it. Artie Kake, the steward, he's a
nice guy, he said he'd resigned himself to
him never eating again until I came along.

HANK *emerges from the kitchenette,*
limping.

HANK: This was the giraffe.

DOLORES: Yes.

HANK: The airforce colonel. He had all his
teeth.

DOLORES: 'Far as I could make out.

HANK *returns to the kitchenette.*
DOLORES *rises and stretches.*
She walks round the room, barefoot.
She sees the mirror and checks her
appearance in it.
She likes what she sees.
She adjusts her new dress.
She turns and looks over her shoulder into
the mirror.
She stretches the back of the dress over her
butt.
HANK *emerges from the kitchenette and*
sees this.
He holds a bowl full of salad.
DOLORES *runs her hand down the*
profile of her butt.
She stretches the dress tight round her butt.
HANK *swallows hard, feels his gut, and*
pushes it back.
DOLORES *turns and repeats her*

performance with her breasts.
HANK *stuffs his mouth with lettuce.*
*He slams the bowl down on the table and
limps back to the kitchenette.*
DOLORES *eats a leaf of lettuce and
returns to her chair.*

DOLORES: The vet was treating Spotty
today. Mrs Operkl's dog? Had an hour's
psychoanalysis. Y'know what she dresses
him in?

HANK (*in the kitchenette*): What.

DOLORES: Two small pairs of designer
jeans and a tee-shirt which says 'Nuke
em'. Artie said I should keep away from
Spotty. Which is why I was sent up a tree.
I caught a glimpse of him from up the
tree. He's so ugly.

HANK *emerges from the kitchenette with
two steaks, cooked, on plates. He places
them on the table.*

HANK: You see much of this Artie?

DOLORES: He's my boss.

HANK: How old is he?

DOLORES *rises and walks to the table.*

DOLORES: Twenny-five? I dunno. He's
young.

HANK *and* DOLORES *sit at the table.*

HANK: Is he married?

DOLORES: No.

They eat their steaks.
HANK *has recourse to nurse his foot
occasionally, under the table.*
DOLORES *speaks as she eats.*

DOLORES: Me and Susan are growing
apart. She can't handle my new-found
wealth. It was OK when I was the
underdog but now I'm successful she's
gone bitchy. She seldom smiles these
days. You remember how she was always
so jolly?
I took her a bunch of flowers yesterday
and they were not on display when I
called by this afternoon. I poked around
in their trash when I left and there were
the flowers, underneath the skeleton of
last night's fish. I went out of my way to
choose their favourite brand so it's not as
if they find 'em offensive, or consider
them to be unlucky like the peacock
feathers they threw out after Judd's Mom
and Dad were killed in their car smash.

I'm gonna tackle Susan head on over this.
I'm gonna ask her what happened to the
flowers? And if she says they wilted or
attracted hornets or some such excuse
like that I'll say I saw 'em in the garbage
and it's plain to me they never reached
display because the nite I called by with
the flowers you was cookin fish and were
about to eat it when I left and the flowers
were beneath the fish remains in the trash
the next day when I departed and that
proves they were thrown out before you
ever sat down to eat your goddam fish!
Of course, I run the risk of Susan askin
what the hell were you doin pokin your
snout into our garbage? Then I will blurt
out an accusation of hardened attitudes
towards me and she will deny it. She'll
proclaim her affection for me is strong as
ever and I'm imagining things and Judd
will sit in the corner smoking his pipe and
reading his mail-order catalogue while we
have a row, hating all the shouting and
embarrassed by Susan's displays of naked
emotion. Susan will throw the mincer at
me. Or worse, hit me in the eye and I will
storm outa the house kickin over their
trash on my way to the car. That'll be
another buddy down the pan. My best
buddy.

She continues eating.
HANK *is ahead of her.*
*He finishes and pushes his plate to one
side.*
*He takes his foot from under the table and
lifts it up.*
Places his foot on the table next to
DOLORES' *plate.*

HANK: Take a look at my foot.

DOLORES *takes a look at* HANK's *foot.*

DOLORES: So what.

HANK: See anything?

DOLORES *takes a mouthful of steak and
scrutinises* HANK's *foot, chewing.*

DOLORES: I don't see anything.

HANK: I trod on a fork.

DOLORES *takes another look at*
HANK's *foot.*

DOLORES: Shoulda picked it up. It's
called housework.

HANK: The fork was on the table.

DOLORES *takes a final look at* HANK's
foot.

DOLORES: I don't see anything.

HANK: It's painful.

*HANK removes his foot from the table.
He rubs the sole and replaces it under the
table.
DOLORES continues eating.*

DOLORES: What were you doing on the table?

HANK: Surfing.

*DOLORES inspects the table, runs her
fingers under the rim.*

DOLORES: It's bone dry.

HANK: I was practising.

DOLORES: I think it's too early for you to go surfing.

HANK: I didn't.

DOLORES: If you were thinking of it.

HANK: I wasn't.

DOLORES: If you incapacitate yourself practising on the lounge table I don't think the Pacific Ocean is quite the place for you.

HANK: I agree.

DOLORES: Good.

*DOLORES has finished her steak.
She pushes her plate ahead of her and
wipes her mouth.*

DOLORES: That was nice. Thank you.

*HANK takes the plates through to the
kitchenette.
DOLORES re-hangs the mirror on the
wall.
She crosses to the easy chair and replaces
her shoes.
She goes to the mirror and fusses with her
hair.
HANK emerges from the kitchenette.
He crosses to the easy chair.
He sits.
DOLORES heads for the door.*

HANK: Where you goin?

DOLORES: Out.

HANK: Where?

DOLORES: See Susan.

HANK: why?

DOLORES: Confront her over this flower business.

HANK: Why?

DOLORES: Because it's bugging me.

HANK: Can't it wait?

DOLORES: No.

HANK: Til tomorrow?

DOLORES: No.

HANK: Oh.

DOLORES: I'll drive over.

HANK: Right.

DOLORES: I won't be an hour.

HANK: No.

DOLORES: Good.

*She goes.
HANK picks his injured foot up and
places it across his knee. He inspects the
foot closely.*

Scene Three

*Later that evening.
HANK sits in the easy chair.
DOLORES arrives.
DOLORES is drunk.*

DOLORES: So what have you bin saying to Judd?

HANK: Haven't seen him.

DOLORES: Bull's *shit*.

HANK: I waved at him whilst running on the beach a day or two back. He was out there with his metal detector.

DOLORES: You did more than wave.

HANK: Yeah I said hi, maybe.

DOLORES: You stopped off in the junklot, exhausted, for a rest.

HANK: I had run five miles, non-stop, across sand.

DOLORES: You had breath enough to tell Judd and Susan about my antics with the monkey.

HANK is silent.

DOLORES: Well it did the trick. They were of course deeply sympathetic for poor Hank whose wife is nothin more than a monkey-fuckin tramp. Come round any time Hank and sit with us in the junklot. Move in if needs be, when the whore brings her monkeys round. You're contemptuous.

HANK: Musta slipped out in conversation.

DOLORES: It didn't work buster. I put 'em straight.

HANK: You're drunk.

DOLORES: I had some wine.

HANK: So who's contemptuous.

DOLORES: Oh Saint Peter here's never bin drunk. Don't twist it.

HANK: I ain't twistin.

DOLORES: I gotta mind to stop your allowance.

HANK: I wouldn't do that if I were you.

DOLORES: Why not.

HANK: I might just have to sell my story to Hollywood.

DOLORES: I'll get there first.

HANK: They wouldn't believe you.

DOLORES: Well Judd and Susan believe me, that's all I care about. They're back on my team.

HANK: What did you tell 'em?

DOLORES: Let's just say they understand my motives. Let's just say that. Let's just say I managed to fill in a few gaps you left out whilst catching your breath no doubt, let's leave it at that. Let's just say I managed to convince them their *gut reaction* was a wrong one. Let's leave it there shall we? Let's say that.

HANK: What did you say?

DOLORES: I told 'em what a shit you've bin to me these fifteen years. I told 'em what a fuckin shit you've bin. What a snivelling fuckin shit you've bin. (*Kicks off her shoes.*) What a snivelling wretched buddy-poaching shit you are. (*Walking round the room.*) Told 'em what a lazy, self-centred shit you are, (*Goes to the fridge and takes out champagne.*) what an asshole, what an impossible asshole you are, (*Going to kitchenette.*) told em what it's like to live with a pathetic, failed asshole, (*Emerges from kitchenette with a glass, crosses to table.*) told 'em what it's like to live with an asshole-shitting

monster, cleaning up after him for fifteen shitstained years. (*Uncorks champagne and pours herself a glass.*) Tole em the lengths I had to go to make ends meet with this shit and his asshole monkey. (*She sits at table and drinks champagne.*) How's your foot.

HANK: Better.

DOLORES: I told em you've taken to surfin on tables. They found that pathetically funny.

HANK: They would.

DOLORES: Yes I told em you three-sixtied on a fork! We burst out laughing on that one! (*She laughs.*) We pissed ourselves over that one! I told 'em you was limpin round the place with your apron on, maimed by a fuckin fork whilst surfin on a table! (*She laughs.*) They both found that extremely amusing. Even Judd took his pipe out and split his face on that one!

HANK: Only reason he smokes a pipe is so folks can distinguish his face from his ass.

DOLORES: Judd is very handsome.

HANK: Handsome.

DOLORES: Yes.

HANK: That's a new one.

DOLORES: He's in fine physical shape. Surfs like a dolphin.

HANK: With his pipe in his mouth.

DOLORES: I've always said to Susan she's a very lucky girl to have someone like Judd. I said so tonite.

HANK: I'm sure Judd appreciated that.

DOLORES: Oh he tweaked my nipple and stroked my ass like he always does when Susan grinds the coffee.

HANK: You're lucky she didn't have to pick the beans.

DOLORES: You're contemptuous.

HANK: I heard she makes him fuck with his pipe in his mouth for fear she might kiss his ass.

HANK *laughs.*

DOLORES: That isn't funny.

HANK *laughs some more.*

HANK: I find it funny. I find it very funny indeed. That's fuckin hilarious!

DOLORES *throws her champagne over* HANK. *He drips with it.* DOLORES *screams:*

DOLORES: It isn't funny!

DOLORES: Funniest fuckin thing I've heard all year!

DOLORES: Well it's my duty to tell 'em that. Y'know? As their friend, As their best friend. As Judd and Susan's very best friend, and longest friend, its my duty to tell 'em what you say, that you make obscene remarks about 'em behind their backs!

HANK: You tell 'em.

DOLORES: I will tell 'em.

HANK: Tell 'em whatever you like.

DOLORES: I will . . .

HANK: I don't give a fuck . . .

DOLORES: I might just go and tell 'em now . . .

HANK: You go ahead. I'll finish the champagne.

DOLORES: I'll take it with me.

HANK *rises and crosses to the table He picks up the champagne bottle and drinks from the neck.* DOLORES *tries to snatch it back.* HANK *grabs it from her, pulling her over. She loses her balance and falls to the floor.* HANK *kicks her.* DOLORES *screams and gets up. She kicks* HANK *back on the shin.* HANK *grunts and shakes the champagne, squirts her in the face with it.* DOLORES *screams and flails at* HANK *with her arms.* HANK *strides to the back of the room and breaks the bottle across the frigidaire. He turns with the broken neck in his hand.* DOLORES *stops still, suddenly sober.*

HANK: Sober now?

DOLORES: Yes.

HANK *tosses the bottle neck onto the floor.*

HANK: Clean it up.

HANK *crosses to the easy chair.* DOLORES *makes her way to the kitchenette. She returns with a dustpan and brush.*

HANK *sits.* DOLORES *sets about sweeping up the broken glass.* HANK *reads her magazine.*

HANK: The shit they write in these magazines. The absolute garbage they fill 'em with. You gotta be a moron from zonko-land to read this.

He reads it. HANK *speaks as* DOLORES *sweeps.*

HANK: Fancy crap. Waste of talent. Where does all the talent go to these days? The military and the magazines. Where's all the great artists? They're designing F1-11's and stuffing magazines with junk. There's too much military and too many magazines. These magazines are the religious paintings of the Medici's. Fill the people's heads with shit so the military can go fuck over defenceless countries with impunity cus all the people back here are sitting home with their heads stuck in a magazine. The more brain-destroying the magazine the more gungho the military becomes. The more gungho the military, the more piss goes in the magazines. So when the balloon goes up and the bomb drops they won't ever know it happened cus they all willa died long ago from the trash they read in magazines.

DOLORES *has finished sweeping up.*

HANK: Finished?

DOLORES: Yes.

HANK: Take your clothes off.

DOLORES: What?

HANK: I'm gonna 'make love' to you tonite.

DOLORES: You're not gonna touch me.

HANK: I'm gonna tweak your nipple and stroke your ass like Judd.

DOLORES: You're not gonna touch me.

HANK: You like I should break another bottle and grind it in your fuckin face?

DOLORES: You're not gonna touch me.

HANK *rises and goes to the kitchenette.*

DOLORES: You're not gonna touch me tonite or any nite.

HANK *emerges from the kitchenette with the neck of the champagne bottle. He*

positions himself between DOLORES
and the door.

HANK: Take your fuckin clothes off.

DOLORES *starts to undress.*

Scene Four

One hour later.
DOLORES *sits alone, in the easy chair,*
wrapped in a sheet.
It is dark.
The room is lit by moonlite only.
HANK *enters.*
He stands in the doorway to the bedroom.

HANK: Shoulda done it on the beach . . .
shoulda gone to the beach . . . if we'd gone
to the beach . . . took the blanket on the
beach . . . remember that? When we used to
do it on the beach? . . . first summer . . . used
to feel horny all day long, had to wait till
dusk then we'd get under the blanket and do
it right there, on the beach . . . with the
people walkin past and all and we never
gave a goddam, remember that? . . . Dol? . .
. if we'd, gone on the beach . . . like when we
did it on the beach . . . Dol? . . . Dolores? . . .
you awake?

He crosses to the easy chair.

DOLORES: Go away.

HANK *kneels on the floor beside her.*

HANK: Dolores . . .

DOLORES: Don't come near me.

HANK: I'm sorry Dol, I'm sorry, I'm so
sorry. I didn't want it to be like this, I
didn't want it . . .

DOLORES: Go away . . .

HANK *rises.*

HANK: . . . I'm so sorry . . .

DOLORES: Don't speak.

HANK: I'm so fuckin unhappy Dolores . . .

DOLORES: Leave me alone.

HANK: Listen to me . . .

DOLORES: Don't speak.

HANK: I'm so fuckin unhappy.

DOLORES: Go away.

HANK: What did I do?

DOLORES: Leave me alone.

HANK: Tell me.

DOLORES *rises and runs into the*
bedroom.
HANK *sits in the easy chair.*

HANK: Aw shit. Aww, shit. What have I
done?

Silence.
Dawn breaks.
The sun rises.
HANK *sits in the easy chair, staring into*
space.
A door slams out back.
HANK *rises.*
He goes to the frigidaire.
He removes three oranges from the fridge.
Slams the door shut.
He takes the organges to the crusher and
crushes them.
Drinks the result back in one.
Returns to the frigidaire and takes out
another three oranges.
Slams the fridge door and crushes the
oranges.
DOLORES *emerges from the bedroom.*
She is dressed in a very short skirt and tight
pullover.
She looks sexually provocative.
HANK *finishes crushing his oranges.*
He walks to the table with his juice.
Sits at the table.
DOLORES *finds her bag and extracts a*
vanity case from it.
Sits at the table and lays out her make-up.
She stands and applies make-up with the
aid of a hand mirror.
She makes up tarty.
HANK *finishes his drink and crosses to*
the frigidaire.
He opens the fridge door and extracts three
more oranges.
As he passes DOLORES *to the crusher he*
speaks:

HANK: You gonna climb up a tree dressed
like that?

DOLORES: Yes.

HANK: Artie Kake gonna be underneath?

DOLORES: I hope so.

HANK: Huh.

He crushes the oranges.

DOLORES: I want you to go to Mexico and
get us a divorce.

HANK: I don't want no divorce.

DOLORES: It's the last nite I ever spend with you.

HANK: Gonna shack up with Artie.

DOLORES: That's none of your business.

HANK: It's my business.

DOLORES: Send me my divorce papers at the zoo.

HANK: Care of the snake pit.

DOLORES *goes to fridge and grabs herself a yoghurt.*
She goes to the kitchenette and finds herself a spoon.
HANK *has finished crushing his oranges.*
DOLORES *sits at the table.*
HANK *sits at the table.*
DOLORES *peels off the top of her yoghurt and licks the underside of the top.*
She eats one spoonful of yoghurt and places the spoon beside the carton.
She continues with her make-up.

DOLORES: I'll give you the bus fare.

HANK: I don't want it.

DOLORES: I'm already askin myself what it was made me stick with you fifteen years six months and thirteen days. Takes people decades to do that y'know? To look back on a past lover and find not one single trace of what it was attracted 'em together. Years it takes 'em. I'm already lookin at you and searching for what it was. It's gone. I've lost it. After one ugly, pointless, disgusting, fruitless, sleepless nite. It was there, before last nite. Right away in the distance. Through the mists, there was something there. Now there's nothin.

HANK *is eating* DOLORES' *yoghurt.*

DOLORES: I'd be thankful if you'd put that down.

DOLORES *is packing her make-up away.*
HANK *flicks a spoonful of yoghurt across her face.*

DOLORES: That was a childish gesture. That was a childish, pointless gesture.

HANK: How many times did you get up like this when I was out on the road uh?

DOLORES *heads for the kitchenette.*

HANK: How many times! How many times did I walk down that fuckin path? And you'd be in here, tartin up like a fuckin tramp!

DOLORES *emerges from the kitchenette with a towel, she's wiping the yoghurt carefully from her face.*

HANK: Answer me that! How many fuckin times!

HANK *rises and snatches the towel from* DOLORES.

HANK: How many times!

DOLORES: Give that back!

DOLORES *snatches back the towel.*
They have one end each.
She tugs at it.
HANK *doesn't let go.*

HANK: Bust my fuckin ass for you! This is all I get! Fuckin killed myself for you! Fuckin bitch! This is all I get!

DOLORES *hits* HANK *on the side of the face.*
HANK *lets go of the towel.*
He punches DOLORES *in the face.*

HANK: Fifteen fuckin years! This is all I get!

He hits her again.
Blackout.

Scene Five

DOLORES *lies on the table.*
The yoghurt is beside her.
The VET *inspects* DOLORES *closely.*
DOLORES *is covered from ankles to waist with the Indian blanket.*
HANK *is hunched in a corner.*
He looks mean and fiddles nervously with a wooden spatula.

VET: You did all this with your bare hands.

HANK: Yes.

VET: She took some blows.

HANK: What have I done.

VET: You broke her neck. Multiple abrasions around her face, widespread econymoses across her upper torso, intra-cranial haemorrhage, ruptured her spleen, cerebral contusions, you ah, you must be in pretty good shape.

HANK: Is she dead?

VET: Oh yes. She's dead.

HANK: She can't be dead.

VET: I'm no doctor, but believe me if your wife was an elephant she'd be dead.

The VET covers DOLORES with the blanket.
HANK snaps the spatula in two.
The VET hears this and glances at HANK.
He picks the yoghurt off the table.
He sniffs it.

VET: This fresh?

HANK nods.
The VET wipes the spoon with the shirt.
He takes the yoghurt to the easy chair and sits.
He eats as he speaks.

VET: I missed breakfast. I generally breakfast in the canteen. Right by the bat house. But I got your call this morning before I even made it to the bat house and I came straight over. Feelin kinda peckish. I guess I shoulda taken breakfast before I set off. I plan breakfast according to the animals I'm treating that day. I take a squint at the duty list on my way to the canteen past the bat house and if there's a carnivore under my name I eat kidneys and bacon. If there's an omnivore on my round I take a tomato with it. And when I have the good fortune to be called out to castrate a chicken, I get an egg. Good ole English breakfast.

He has finished his yoghurt.
He stands and places the empty carton delicately back where he found it.
He walks to the door.

VET: Your wife had a remarkable gift with animals. We'll miss her at the zoo. Her contribution to Artie's giraffe programme was colossal. I'll sneak out now, and leave you to your bereavement.

The vet sidles out.
HANK stands and walks to the table.
He uncovers DOLORES down to the neck.
He speaks to DOLORES:

HANK: My poor little monkey. My poor, darlin little monkey, I don't know what the hell I'm gonna do without ya. I flicked yoghurt in your face that was stupid wasn't it? Y'know you once said, after the monkey died you said if we ever had children and we told 'em we had a monkey they'd say we know. He's up there lookin down on us. I said that's a sweet thought. If you're up there lookin down Dolore for Chrissakes I dunno what I've done I'm so sorry, I wish to fuck I was up there with ya lookin down on me, if we was both up there lookin down we'd be happy wouldn't we? We'd get along real fine. Are you up there Dolores? Where are you! For fucksake! (*He falls across DOLORES.*) Come back! Come back here! (*Shaking her.*) DOLORES come back! Please, come back. DOLORES come back for Chrissakes! DOLORES! DOLORES!

He slides her off the table and holds her tight, in the centre of the floor, crying her name and swinging her from side to side.
The atmosphere changes.
Music.
They dance.

DOLORES: Hey, I know you, you're the guy who surfs with a monkey on his back . . .

HANK: That's right.

DOLORES: What's your name?

HANK: Hank. Hank Wandaback.

DOLORES: I'm Dolores.

HANK: That's a sweet name.

DOLORES: I hate it.

They dance.

DOLORES: Where's the monkey?

HANK: Right outside, playin in the garden.

DOLORES: Introduce me?

HANK: Maybe we should get to know each other first.

They dance.
HANK smiles.
The lights fade.

BUD

Bud was first performed as part of the Not the RSC Festival at the Gulbenkian Theatre, Newcastle upon Tyne and subsequently at the Almeida Theatre, London in November 1985. The part of Bud was played by Geoffrey Hutchings and the director was Peter Clough.

BUD *and* MYRNA's *kitchen, with table, chairs, rocker, tumble drier.*

BUD: She own this farm see? She own it. 'Ole farm belong to er. Twas er mother's. Now tis ers. And whereas the ownership trump seldom cut across the bows of a joyful marriage, well, look at it this way . . . we git men comin in ere. Drivers for grain, vets. T.B. chaps, EEC wallahs, wool merchants; tree surgeon she ad in once, egg chap once a week. Diesel geezer. And not once ave she chose to stand up in this ere kitchen, an broach with a stranger this farm dun't belong to Bud ere, it belong to me. Not once. She id'n no eyebrow raiser. She could. She could come right out with it to any bugger who come in ere, but she dun't. But I never demanded on condition a marriage that she relinquish ownership to me an she respect that. Myrna's older'n me. Decade senior. So I said to meself no Bud you can't make a demand on Myrna like 'at. Older woman, respect for age. The other reason is she worked this place single-damn-anded for a full two decades 'fore I set foot across the yard gate. Twas a combination of creepin arthritis on er part, and desire on mine that brung we together an nothin else. There's people in this vicinity – not Lady Rickeard who own the estate what border on the farm, but more the bastard shitkickers over Rumford way where the topsoil's thinner, the moorland bog people, broad horizon narrer mind, the chapel parrots who after two decades of happy, peaceful marriage, *still* maintain I married er for er bloody farm. An they still yak that and I knew that for a fact cus er sister Sonya's one of em. She's the one who keep the empty gossip bottle drippin acid. Acid. Gnawin away, eatin away at my wife's better judgement. I have never, in two harmonious, blissful decades a marriage, posted one iota of an idea in her ead about a Will, or oo it go to, or any other testate like at. Or otherwise. So that put e in the picture so far as Myrna and ownership a the property is concerned. Now iss all come to ead wi' this dutch barn. It go back further'n that, before lady Rickeard dropped in the first time ever on er orse. We got li'l acid drops scorchin oles in the startched napkin of our marriage stretchin back sempteen year to the arrival of the sheddist . . . but right now tis the dutch barn.

Christ almighty! (*He throws a cigarette packet across the table.*) Tis fower legs an a ruddy roof! Thass all it is! Fower stantions and a gable! Bugger id'n gonna lay an egg! I ad a fower-legged chicken, laid like a machine. Like a machine. Myrna didn' like it; said tid'n natural. I said Christ almighty if I injected you with overdose a testosterone you a sprout more'n fower legs! Bugger lay like a machine she dun't gallop like orse! Fower-legged chicken was a needle nothin more cus I knew I was in the right on that one. Eggs is my gamble. My investment. Cus I reckon the EEC's gotta come down wi' big subsidies on eggs sooner or later. They got no egg reserve anyplace in Europe an eggs is in big decline. So I got olda all these dicky – dodgy, birds, oo've ad overdose, cheap, wi' fower legs, three wings, two eads, bloody equipment there you'd never occasion on a hen – but the buggers lay like there's no tomorrer. So twas a needle . . . but the day Lady Rickeard dropped in, first time, ever. That was the bombshell. Myrna'n me was in ere. I'd bin out ploughin an was back ome eatin crib, an Myrna ad a corn bag on er knee pluckin a chicken. Yes twas Myrna. I knaw poultry's my li'l empire in all this, but on this occasion Myrna'd said to me, Bud I can't stand to see that fower-legged chicken oppin round the mowey no more, you gotta slaughter it. I said that bloody chicken's layin like automatic – an she was – bambambambambam eggeggeggeggeggegg. Couldn' stop er. So I said, Myrna you want that chicken you wring er neck you pluck it you boil'n up. Cus I arn't touchin of her till she ease up layin. So thass why twas Myrna sat there, bang on that seat there, pluckin a chicken, alf-plucked chicken, feathers on the floor, knock knock on the door. I'll go Myrna . . . Tis Lady Rickeard, Myrna. Christ Almighty! Whass she got on? Thass the first damn thing come into er ead. Whass she got on? Britches an a whip. That all? She's on a bloody orse! So, Myrna panic. Quick as a flash she open up the tumble drier, this one ere, an in go the chicken, the corn bag, an all the feathers she could muster. She slam the door shut, an outa force a pure abit, switch the bugger on. So in walk Lady

Rickeard to the picture of 'alf-plucked chicken tumbling round the tumble drier wi' me an Myrna mesmerised to it like a snake an two rats. Lady Rickeard's eyes is swivellin with the chicken tryin to adjust emselves to believe what it is they're lookin at when I break the ice by offering er a whiskey. To Myrna's distaste she accepted an first off she was polite. Very Nice Person. Could I leave my orse outside? Myrna said we'd prefer she didn' bring it in, outa all sincerity cus we'm none of us sure round ere a what's acepted be'aviour up there on the estate, but I laughed it off an said we got a dead cow in the mowey, contracted meningitis and dropped dead, we'm waitin for the council . . . Good eavens she said, Efty's sid a dead cow before now. Silence. 'Cept for the drier. Bloody drier. Whaddaya do leave er tumble? Or switch er off an call attention to it. There's a very slim chance she might notta noticed. Anyhow. Nice name for orse though Bud. Efty. Thass Myrna. Makin conversation. 'Named him Hefty after my husband, Hugh. I called Hugh Hefty because, well he was, for years. Then Hefty came along and Hugh said call him Hefty. And do you know I haven't called Hugh Hefty since Hefty came alone?' I thought to meself my Christ almighty this is personal. This is a lady, Nobility, tellin we what she call er usband when they'm orizontal. She gotta be after summin. On the want. This is boilin up to nothin shorta discrepancy over land. This is boundary talk, this is. Turned out I was bang on target. Bullseyed in one.

But we gotta go back. It all start sempteen year ago on our third, passionate wedding anniversary. I was way out a mile off taggin sheep in the twelve acres, on the hill. Tis on that stand point you can see for miles over the farm an across the moor, I could just pick out through squintin eyes, the first firework in our wedded bliss, walkin in a dead straight line towards me. An the bugger's bin sparkin an splutterin ever since.

He moves to table and takes a paper from the drawer; reads.

'I am a sheddist. Outcast. Monkish. Trapped. I live off home-grown weeds and strangled cats. The diet of an exile. My birthplace slips and slithers towards the sea, slowly, perceptible to only those who want to see, and we are banished to the safer side, on solid ground, beyond the rotting earth we call our home and safe. And sad. Sound, but yearning with a pounding heart to leap across the border, back and free to warn again. I built my shed from rotting planks and woodwormed wood I scavenged from the exiled dead. I will die too, when the time comes. What will be left but me? And a row of skulls on fingerbones, staring out to sea.'

BUD *lowers the paper.*

Now dun' ask me what it mean, but that to me is the product of a first-rate mind. Goddam bastard poet. Of the finest kilter.

He reads again.

'Signed, the Sheddist. PS, would you be so kind as to hang these plants upside down in your airing cupboard till they are dry.'

I'll explain that, an all the rest ob'm, (*Holding up a huge wad of papers from the drawer*) later. But that was writ be the man who now assailed me in the twelve acres as I tagged me last sheep. E said, I'm on a lay line bud. E didnt knaw my name was Bud, e coulda called me skip, or mister, but e chose to call me bud. I'd never sid'n ever before. E said this ere lay line's weakenin be the minute. E said I'll shortly reach the end. E said I bin walkin scores a miles in a dead straight line, an now I'm near the end. E said tis 'ighly unusual to reach the end of a lay line. E said I wanna build a shed e said, on the end a this ere lay line. A shed I said. Yes e said. A shed. We was right on the edge of the wood by now, on top of the ill. Wallop, ere, e said. On the edge. A shed. Damme ta hell. To live in? Oh yes e said. Quite alone. Well I took to the man. E was quiet. E was a sad man. E was determined, like the way e walked on a dead straight line over buildins, through hedges, across rivers, dead straight along this layline for Christ, miles. Score upon score upon scores a miles. E slept in gateways where cows give birth. E was well spoken. I never asked'n oo e was, where e come from, nothin, cept e musta come from th'other end a this ere lay line an I coulda found out by devious means where that was but damme you gotta give way to intuition when it 'ounds ya an bugger me I was beset with it over this chap. A voice inside my head yelled out to me Bud This Is A Man From Another Time OO Want Is Corner Of England, His End Of A Lay Line, Where No Bastard's Gonna Come An Lay Trouble On Is Doorstep. Submit! E built is shed on stilts, nestled in the edge of the trees lookin out across the field, outa wood out the wood. An I think I've laid eyes on'n twice in the past sempteen years. But every week once a week there's bin a note of this ere writin pinned on our door, with a buncha these ere plants, green plants, wi' big leaves, for we to dry. We dry em out in the rayburn alcove, an I carry em out the implement shed an lay em on the baler. They'm always gone when I go there next. But we never see'n. Myrna's never seed'n. But back to day one.

'You dun't knaw oo e is, where e comes from, is name, e could be any bugger. E could be murderer, IRA, Horse Maimer, Cattle stealer, and ere e is set up shop on *MY LAND!*'

An there it was. After three years of sweet adoration, blowed right up in my face. The question of ownership. I was shocked. Tell me this: if, at any time, it ad entered my ead, that I wed Myrna for her farm alone, that there should be one iota of motive ulterior to the love an respect I bore that woman, for weddin er, would I have stood ground on the Sheddist issue? And staked my name on er will against the principle of allowin a man to build a shed on a useless corner a woodland because pure an simple that is where he desired above all to be? Aw Myrna. You are lucky my darlin. You are lucky, my dearest cherry ripe, that you have never had to live without collateral. And your hysterial overtones in response to this man confirm my suspicion that those born with collateral are sterile in compassion! Like the fower-legged chicken, later on I said if you wanna tell'n to sling is ook, you take the axe to the stilts of is shed an bring it down round is ears, cus I ain't. She left'n be. Seethed for a while. Simmerd after that, then slowly clicked back into the cogs of a well-greased marriage. But every now an again, she needled, where before she never needled. The chicken was the first one. The first subtle reminder of oo own the land. First needle. Never a lump ammer to bruise the skin, always a needle, to prick it. Twas my idea, last arvest, to build a dutch barn, when I was out there settin fire to all this straw. I said, to meself, why not erect a dutch barn Bud? I could bale'n up, put'n in there. Pure an applied logic. So I drawed up the plans, (*Indicates cigarette box.*) briefed meself on the ins an outs, whys an wherefores, an one night presented the evidence in favour before Myrna. Fait accompli. She stood up, paced the floor. An said Brod'rick. Were you aware that sheep meat is expected to top 295,000 tonnes? Er, no Myrna. Christ I adn'n expected this. And that surplus purchase garuntees on grade two barley are likely to be withdrawn within the next five year? If unemployment rise an there's a concomitant increase in the sale a beer? Cherry Ripe, I arn't altogether sure that can be relied on, if you refer to recent statistics on the subject, I said. And projected computer assessments over the same period, there's a wide discrepancy. She rejoined by statin that the computer figures was based on the inaccurate belief that in times of wholesale stress such as that induced by widespread unemployment, tis the consumption a spirits what increase, at the expense of ale an weak beer, Brod'rick, an that computer eb'm bin programmed to taste the difference. At this point I rolled me eyes to the backa me ead an paused to reappraise meself a the debate so far and found to my delight that Myrna ad bin arguin my case! I put this to er and she replied with a whiplash. Tis the barely eads what brew the beer Brod'rick, burn the blimmin straw!

Now that, is code, for Myrna sayin to me – I own this farm. I ave all the ideas round ere. If *I* wanna build a dutch barn you build it, if *you* wanna build a dutch barn, I squash it.

And in the absence of any discussion whatsoever on the taboo subject of the sheddist, thass the way these needles d'come out. And prick. See she believed me to begin with. She believed. I come to Myrna twenny one year ago, I said Myrna you'm alone. I'm alone. I gotta respect for ya. I'm ten years younger'n you. But I arn't fussed about that. Ow about a year's courtin, then marriage. Tis too late for children, so there's no rush, then after twelve month we'll wed, an I'll move in. Keep it legal an respectable. So to my relief, she agreed, and we courted, and fell in love. What started out as what might seem to you a cold-blooded proposition, turned into a passionate love affair, as these things often do. On a slow afternoon in September we beached ourselves and netted a few big silver fish, talked of old pals who'd joined th Navy, or emigrated, or wed. We lingered on the pals oo'd wed, and reflected ow for many their life-long partnerships ad started out as passionate love affairs, and ended up as cold-blooded propositions. Awww, my Christ, ow we ad the upper and on them. Ow we wished to see em see us by the sea. See em gaze at we. Me an Myrna. My darlin Cherry Ripe. What is it a man a thirty sees in a forty year old woman with arthritis? Thass what the chapel parrots was askin. It can't be love. Can't be lust. Can't be passion. Can't even be enthusiasm. Gotta be collateral. But apart from the odd rash deed, when I've acted on nothin more'n intuition, I've always bin a sit and wait man. Got left behind, when all the pals paired up an wed, got marked down for a bachelor, but that never bugged me. Nothin ever bugged me, cus I burn on a slow fuse. And tis the slow fuses what crop up with the most unexpected bangs. They're the least understood. Cus they dun't operate like no-one else. Hence Myrna. But her sister Sonya wouldn' buy that. She's no fool. She dug in, cus she's my age Sonya, an as expected all er life when Myrna kicks the bucket this farm will be Sonya's. At £2,000 an acre thass a round quarter million Myrna's sittin on ere, an thass collateral that is. Aw yeah. Quarter million. Thass the sums we'm jugglin with. An when you reckon you bin pre-empted on that kinda collateral, you dun't ang round discussin why. Or how. You go to war. War of attrition, and er propaganda's wicked. Barbed. It stick. On Myrna. And over the years, Myrna's come to believe it. Slow. Imperceptible, Sonya's built, brick upon brick, brick upon brick, sidled up an piled it on, a wall between us. All founded on that one li'l naggin doubt, that needle, was e sincere? Do e love is misses? Does Bud love Myrna like e said e did? Or is e after collateral? And every bastard time she say 'I own this Farm', 'No Dutch Barn', 'That Soddin Sheddist'. She mean dun't you count your fower-legged chickens before the buggers 'atch Brod'rick Cramb. I'm gonna keep you guessin. Why did you marry me Bud Cramb? I married ya cus I loved ya! I love ya! I love ya! I love ya! I love ya! Why can't a man love a woman ten year older'n e? With arthritis. Why is it money! Money! Ya stupid lousy bitch Cherry Ripe open up your eyes! See what they're doin to us! Look at me! Am I lyin now? Am I? Trust me! For Chrissake Myrna what have I gotta do! What is left for me to say? I dun't care about the bastard Collaterall! Collateral can fly to the edga hell! Sell it all up! Give it all away! Give it to Sonya I don't give a bullock's tongue so long as our years are happy an my memories of you are happy bloody memories! Thass all. Thass all in the world I swear what occupy my mind behind ere. No grudge. No hatred. No malice. No hope of an early death an a quick killin. Thass all there is Cherry Ripe.

BUD *sits on the chair opposite the tumble driver, and stares at it.*

Forgive me askin this, am I seein things, or does that chicken ave four legs? Which chicken would that be Lady Rickeard? The chicken in your tumble drier. Oh, That chicken. Yes, as a matter a fact, it has. And how often do you cook them in the tumble drier? Every Thursday. When tis time to pluck em. I see.

Lies, lies, lies. Aw Myrna. Why can't you say See Lady Rickeard, I was pluckin the chicken in the kitchen on account of if I do it out in the barn in the cold like this it get old a my arthritis and me fingers go stiff. Then you come over on your orse, and I panic cus I don't want you ta think . . . thass all it take . . .

Were you aware the Forestry Commission is sellin off its assetts? Oh yes Lady Rickeard. Oh yes. £600 an acre, tis a bargain. Why they gotta strip a woodland up there, sixty acres . . : I've bought it. Thass an eyebrow raiser. That li'l gem raised fower eyebrows. Two a Myrna's, an two a mine. Myrna's damn near 'it the roof. When they dropped they 'it the plancheon. I beg your pardon Lady Rickeard? We've bought it. Hugh and I, with a syndicate. We intend to breed pheasants and shoot them. There are six of us. Quite sensitive people, sensitive in the respect that they are, politically sensitive. Members of parliament, judiciary, and so forth. Oh yes? Of course that's not all. There will be guests, paying guests, equally sensitive, throughout the season, weekending, and so forth. I see. What I came to speak to you about, we er, have inspected the woodland, toured its boundaries and so forth, with our gamekeeper and, people. Yes? There's the question of the man who lives in the hut. Was he granted planning permission do you know? To build it? Iss bin there sempteen year. I see. If a place've bin built five year they can't touch ya. Id'n that so Lady Rickeard? Yes, I believe it is. That was me talkin to er. I could see what she was gettin at. E's lived there sempteen years Lady Rickeard. E's never bin any trouble to we, in fact we never see'n from one year's end to the next. A recluse . . . Does he pay you rent? Oh no. Nothin at all. E's, e's a good chap. E won't pinch your pheasants. E wun't get in your way, e wun't do nothin. Damme twill be like e id'n there. You ave my word for that, Lady Rickeard. My intuition. I didn't say that, bout the intuition, it might weaken the argument. Cus she sure as ell wanted to get rid ob'm. She ad'n said as much but intuition tole me that. An intuition proved right again. Intuition leapt screamin out and landed legs up on the plancheon, gaspin for recognition after er next gem, but I didn' let on. 'Bout the intuition. I've kept intuition to meself, right since when I was a tacker when I first knew I possessed the stuff. Intuition is a rare gift. Gotta be kept outa sight. Tis intuition first put me onta Sonya, an the chapel parrots. Yeah. Intuition got collateral beat. Gimme intuition anyday. An I telle summin. I ab'm met that many collateral wallahs oo got more'n a fingernail of intuition. Damme I can fart pints a the stuff an still be left wi' plenty.

I don't think you quite understand. The man is a security risk. He's, he's been checked on, she said, an they reckon it's possible he's part of a terrorist organisation, a syndicate. That was unfortunate choice a word, seein ow she'd juss used it to describe er own crowd. Syndicate. Anyhow, she ad more to say. He has a criminal record, she said. E's a trafficker in drugs, he was convicted of possession and transaction of cannabis. Christ almighty. My eyes shifted to the bloody Rayburn, an sure enough there was a buncha them damn plants. Cannabis! Thass what it was! Fuck me gently I said, more outa shock than as a prelude to anythin in particular. I stumbled, e, e, musta bin convicted over sempteen years ago I said. Yes this was in 1966 replied Lady Rickeard. She ad all the facts at er fingertips. She'd done er omework. As e committed any other crime? Asked Myrna. Not that we know of, yet. Said Lady Rickeard. But I have it on the very highest authority that he is a security risk. Thass a pity thun Lady Rickeard. You'll ave to go an shoot your pheasants elsewhere. This time it was my eyebrows that bounced off the roof an it the plancheon, cus that wad'n me oo said that. Twas bloody Myrna! She was defendin er sworn buggerin enemy 'gainst nobility! She'd stood up be now and rounded on er ladyship an this gived me the opportunity to go an stuff the cannabis in the rayburn. That there is my land, she was sayin to er ladyship, an I can do what the hell I like with it! Thass land anded down to me from my mother an iss bin in this family for years, long before your crowd come along and pitched their ruddy orse boxes all over other people's small 'oldins! An I got collateral. You can't touch me. I'm in the black wi' collateral. So you git on 'efty an hoof off outa here! Summin musta touched a nerve in Myrna, cus Lady Rickeard ad bin most polite in all this. Icy, slightly icy, yes, but the picture a dignity. An Myrna respect these superficialities of protocol more'n I do. Intuition tole me a nerve ad bin battered raw with a lump ammer someplace, an the affair ad'n ended ere, it'd only juss begun.

Soon as Myrna shut the door on Lady Rickeard she stormed back in the kitchen and shut off the tumble drier. Silence. Apart from a thud as the dessicated bird hit the floor of the damn dryer. Now suppose you tell me what the hell that man's doin ere? A convicted criminal! Growin drugs, on *MY FARM*, usin we as accessories? That had, I must confess, knocked a dent in my intuition. That ad blown a big ole in my intuition. Never would I ave guessed I was talkin to a criminal. Thass what e was, in the eyes a some, includin Myrna. E shoulda come clean on that one. An as for givin it to we to dry out for'n, thass buggerin barefaced cheek that is. No I wad'n feelin so protective towards matey up the shed by now, an I was damned quizzical as to why Myrna'd stuck up for'n. Cus I wouldna. Not after that. Christ thass the first time intuition let me down. An thass the trouble with intuition, if it let ya down, juss once, then it cease to be intuition. Take a damn lifetime. Sempteen ruddy year e oodwinked me, that bastard. Up there, gettin 'igh, not a care in the bollockin world, wi me down ere battin ard for'n on a sticky bloody wicket. Cus tis more'n that tis a bollockin minefield. This collateral, oo own what, cohabitation, tis a ruddy whirlpool, suckin ye down, down, and iss knocked years off me. Look at me. Bloody fifty year old, look at me. Shakin like a leaf! All for that bastard up there! Intuition, be buggered. No matter ow long you d'work wi' somebody. Ow long y'live with em . . . Years . . . Decades. There's gotta be a moment in time, when they d'spring summin on ya, that make y'ask the question did I ever knaw er at all? Thraw all the safe knowledge you stored up about em, like grain, outa kilter. All the li'l abits that get e from one milestone to another throughout the day, all the props they set there t'old e up cut out from under ya. All in the space a time it take y'to say 'then you'll ave to go an shoot your pheasants elsewhere Lady Rickeard.' Thass time playin tricks for ya. Two decades up in smoke in the space a two, three seconds. Turns out Sonya's never spoke a word to Myrna 'bout the collateral. Never a whisper. Thass news to me. Turned out she never even go chapel. Sonya. Not no more. Stopped chapel fifteen year ago. All in the mind, see. So oo put it up ther thun? Up ther? In the mind? Twad'n Sonya. We cannot rely on it being Sonya no more. Was it me? Why *did* I marry Myrna? Was my love for Myrna conditioned somehow, by an unconscious lust for er collateral. An ow did that lust manifest itself? Ow much did Myrna suspect or guess? Much. Much much. She positively nurtured it. Poured bag upon bag a Fisons 365 on that li'l nettle. Hence the four-legged chicken scat an that. She knew I never loved er, from day damn one. Twas the collateral I was after all the time, an the only bastard oo didn' knaw it was me.

I bin thinking Bud. Bout that dutch barn. To git back to that ruddy dutch barn. I bin thinkin I might erect it meself. Well Myrna, what about y'arthritis? Oh Bud, arthritis id'n that bad. If I d'wear gloves I a git by. Why can't I elp ya? Aw you dun't wanna put yourself out Bud, thought I a do it in me own time, twill be summin to git me through the winter. Make a change from knittin. Tis the knittin what brung on the arthritis. I consulted me dutch barn plan. (*He looks at cigarette packet.*) Myrna the stantions are leb'm metres igh. Big RSJ's, six ob'm. You gotta set they in concrete, dead perpendicular, thass before you start the roof. Ow're you gonna manage that? 'Tractor'n gib'. Quick as a dash. She'd gived it thought. Twad'n impulse. Calculated humiliation. Sittin there in front of the tumble dryer, in the kitchen I a shared with er for two damn decades. I got the strength Bud. Remember, I worked this farm single-anded before you come along. Yes. Yes. Yes Myrna. Strength. Thass all thass left in the end. When you git to the end a the lay line like me an Myrna ave, it all boil down to strength. She ad the sinews of a – I was gonna say chicken. Yeah; chicken. Ad muscles on her like rock. Bloody arm muscles up there. Rock. But in the end, when the mind's, whacked out, spent. When the brain's bin knotted up an shrivelled like gristle. There's no more, whass the word, outlet. Tis just weighin down on ya, like a weight, what is it, revenge. Revenge revenge revenge. Tis a filthy word, revenge. Hard relentless word, go on for ever. Revenge. An there's nothin beyond it. She played wi' me thass all she did. Thass all I was there for. Did'n need me. She eld every single card in the pack. Twas like I was er bloody wife. Juss brung in to scrub this an pluck that. For er amusement. Entertainment. Comp'ny. Any bugger woulda done an in the end it boil down to strength. Bein ten years younger was a, advantage. Bein a man. Funny tis the first time I ever thought of us as bein different in that way. Not in er, y'knaw in bed an all that but, in relation to what we did y'knaw, ow we ah, allocated. Allocated tasks an that . . . never come into it. But it. Y'knaw it come down to it in the end. When twas a battle in the end of strength. Strength is ah, tis like revenge like when it git olda ya thass all there is. Thass the last resort an tis the last resort cus there's nothin left an tis there. I d'knaw. I d'knaw no more. Dutch barn anyhow, she started on that. An she built the bastard thing. Single damn anded. An twas there, every time I went out the bloody door in the mowey, right where the cow ad meningitis. Standin there a bloody monument. Laughin at me, for bein such a damn simple fool. 'Magine what the goddam chapel parrots a made a me, tis all there in that dutch barn. An she come in there, sat down there one day, smacked er ands an said tis finished. She was tired. In er chair. I ad the oven gloves, in me 'ands, like that, an I juss put em round er neck an pulled. I strangled er, an, that was it. Easier'n wringin a chicken's neck. Strength see. Thass all it boil down to. Strength.